Mother Courage and Her Children

Works of Bertolt Brecht
published by
Arcade

The Caucasian Chalk Circle

The Good Person of Setzuan, adapted by Tony Kushner

The Good Person of Szechwan

The Good Person of Szechwan, Mother Courage and Her Children,
and *Fear and Misery of the Third Reich*

Life of Galileo

Life of Galileo, The Resistible Rise of Arturo Ui,
and *The Caucasian Chalk Circle*

Mother Courage and Her Children

Mother Courage and Her Children, adapted by David Hare

Mr. Puntila and His Man Matti

The Rise and Fall of the City of Mahagonny
and *The Seven Deadly Sins of the Petty Bourgeoisie*

The Threepenny Opera

The Threepenny Opera, Baal, and *The Mother*

BERTOLT BRECHT

Mother Courage and Her Children

a new version by **David Hare**

ARCADE PUBLISHING • NEW YORK

FIRST ARCADE PAPERBACK EDITION 1996

Mother Courage and Her Children was originally published in German under the
title *Mutter Courage und ihre Kinder*. This version by David Hare premiered at
the National Theatre in London, England, in November 1995 and was first
published in Great Britain by Methuen Drama.

Library of Congress Cataloging-in-Publication Data

Brecht, Bertolt, 1898–1956.
     [Mutter Courage und ihre Kinder. English]
     Mother Courage and her children / Bertolt Brecht : a version for the
National Theatre by David Hare. — 1st Arcade pbk. ed.
     p. cm.
     ISBN 1–55970-361-X
     I. Hare, David, 1947–   . II. Title.
PT2603.R397M82 1996
832'.912 — dc20   96-30524

Published in the United States by Arcade Publishing, Inc., New York
Distributed by Little, Brown and Company

10 9 8 7 6 5 4 3 2 1

CCP

PRINTED IN THE UNITED STATES OF AMERICA

Contents

Introduction

The first play of Brecht's that I translated was *The Mother*.
The immediate result was not good, for I kept too close to
the original. This is certainly the main difficulty for Brecht
translators. If they love Brecht – and presumably only
those who do translate him – they try to copy the play in
their own language. They want to be as faithful as possible
– and then nothing comes of it.

Ruth Berlau

Anyone reading the critical commentary on *Mother Courage*
quickly realises that it is beset with the same fruitless
academic questions that are asked about *The Life of Galileo*.
Written at the same time, and set in the same period –
though in a very different part of Europe – *Mother Courage*
invites the same type of speculation. Is it a real tragedy? Is
the central character intended to be sympathetic or is she
alienating? Is she a symbol of the indomitable spirit of
universal motherhood, or is she a blind scavenger putting
money and profit above anything else? To what degree are
we meant to identify with her? Are we 'allowed' to feel for
her?

When Jonathan Kent directed *The Life of Galileo* in 1994 at
the Almeida, the audience watching Richard Griffiths'
beautiful performance as Galileo knew how pointless it was
to worry about the issues which exercise Brecht's critics.
Such questions, to some extent, even confused Brecht's
reactions to productions of his own play. He himself
remarked that if people laid aside their idea of his theoretical
writings and instead turned their attention to the works
themselves, then they might find them less forbidding than
they imagined.

It quickly becomes plain when presenting *The Life of
Galileo* in a real playhouse that if the producer and actors
uncover the actions and essential thought of the play, it is

irrelevant to ask whether Galileo should 'move' you or not by his awareness of his own cowardice. In the same way, it is pointless to worry in the abstract whether the effect of a performance of *Mother Courage* may be overly sentimental, or overly harsh. The worst possible way of approaching the play is to ask only whether the central character is admirable or despicable. The point is not simply what we may *feel* about her opportunism. It is to watch how brilliantly Brecht shows the effects of that opportunism on events, and of events on that opportunism.

What the two plays have in common is that they are both portraits of extremely clever people. It is usually said, in a rather condescending way, that Mother Courage has a sort of 'peasant' wisdom (as if this were generically different from your wisdom and mine, and slightly belonging to the crafty world of gnarled old woodfolk or Arab street traders). But in fact she is far more of a *petit bourgeois* than a peasant. She is in trade, and for a good part of the play, quite successfully. Her wisdom is that of someone who is naturally very brilliant.

In the play Brecht says: suppose you went into a war, and you happened to be one of the cleverest people in the world, and you had developed the most sophisticated possible strategy for protecting yourself against the hurt that war might do you – if, in fact, you were clear-eyed about the purpose and meaning of that war, and how to survive in it – what good would your lucidity be to you? And he comes back with the resounding answer: none. It scarcely matters what way you choose to behave in a war. It will reach you and destroy you whichever way you think about it. It destroys the brave (Eilif), the saintly (Kattrin) and the stupid (Swiss Cheese) alike.

At the beginning Mother Courage seeks the war out. She is not in any sense an innocent victim. On the contrary, she travels to Scandinavia to take part in one war (the Polish–Danish War) long before she moves on to the main conflict (the Thirty Years War) in which the play is generally understood to be set. She goes in order to make a living, and armed with a view of things which at this point she believes will see her through. But the whole point of the play is to show the process whereby this acuteness in her becomes redundant, sick and finally absurd.

Mother Courage finds a war, joins it, goes over to the other side (the Catholics) and then prospers. While she prospers, her philosophy is at its most witty, confident and astute. Yet as the war grinds on, and her children are taken from her, and she crosses back over to her original side (the Protestants), so poverty and waste rob her of the ability to speak about what is happening to her. As the play progresses, and the bodies pile up, her cleverness no longer fits the situation. Her dazzling insights about the nature of war come to seem harsher and more irrelevant. Her brilliance becomes a perverse kind of craziness, stubborn, defiant and self-willed. But if her way of coping no longer seems adequate, whose does? Kattrin's heroic resistance, though successful at one level – the town is woken – also results in her own death.

If I were to propose an alternative title for the play, it would be 'The Silencing of Mother Courage'. In arguing this, I would stress that part of this silencing is, obviously, self-imposed. Alongside *Galileo*, this is one of Brecht's two great masterpieces on the subject of cowardice and assimilation. It goes without saying that Mother Courage's collaboration in the war appals us. So does her dog-eat-dog approach to life in general. One of Brecht's overriding purposes in writing the play is to show that without the complicity of people like Mother Courage, wars would be much harder for generals to undertake. In Scene Four, her philosophy of survival involves her telling soldiers that it is useless to protest, that anger is a waste of time. There is never anything to be gained by making a fuss. And in the hideous Scene Seven – when she is at her most affluent – her more brutal thoughts about the profits to be made from war have a ghastly, triumphalist ring. But the fascinating balance of this work comes from Brecht also showing that a great part of the silencing is imposed by events.

Although Brecht claimed that the play was not formally structured – it is intentionally more like a series of illustrations – it does, however, have an overall shape and one which is very elegant. It opens with a mother being separated from one of her children for the first time. It ends when all three of them are dead. Between these two events, the development of the play is shaped not just by the obvious physical images of a woman becoming ever more isolated as she loses the family and friends who pull her cart, but also by the way she says less and less as the play goes on. In a stunning coup at the end, everyone else sings, *and she is, at last, silent*. The person who has had a view about everything now has a view about nothing.

In her silences, Mother Courage knows full well the cost of her actions. Nothing is more moving than when she says 'Maybe I haggled too long' before Swiss Cheese's death. But it is only moving because, although she has precipitated the death of her own son, she now has no alternative but silently to accept that cost. Once she is in the war, and once she feeds it with her children's presence, then she, like everyone else, is mown down by the war's vile logic. Like most of us, trying to be clever – how often that word comes up in the play, and how uselessly! – Mother Courage does terrible things. Like most of us, she knows she is doing them.

There is, however, one significant way in which this play is very different from the other great work of Brecht's exile. *The Life of Galileo* is, in the best sense, an intellectual play. Its development is through thought, through the movement of ideas – in fact, through speech. *Mother Courage*, on the contrary, is propelled through action. This is hardly surprising. Since it is sometimes making familiar Marxist points that what you believe depends on where you find yourself in the system – a Marxist puts it that your ideology is the product of your social status, and not vice versa – so inevitably it shows belief itself as being relative. But, more than that, belief becomes a kind of effluent, the stuff people cheer themselves up with while history kicks them in the teeth. A wonderful, repeated image of the play is of everyone sitting round having a nice chat, an interlude, while history takes a breather. But it's never for long. When the Chaplain says war's not too bad, because we can still stop for a shit or a meal, he is completely wrong. Because war is then seen to resume with renewed savagery.

It is always said glibly of *The Life of Galileo* that its principal character is not the astronomer, but the People. Even after a year working on a new version of the play, I never quite knew what Eric Bentley meant by saying this. Had it indeed been Brecht's intention, then I am not sure he successfully realised it. But, in *Mother Courage*, two of the principal characters are indeed abstract nouns. They are Time and War. In their turn, they are attended by a flotilla of minor characters called Grief, Waste, Money, Religion and so on. One of the main jobs of a director approaching *Mother Courage* is to find a way of embodying Time and War, so he can show what they do to Mother Courage herself.

David Hare, 1995

Production history

Mother Courage was written in the autumn of 1939 during
Brecht's Swedish exile on Lidingo Island. He was forty.
Although Brecht had originally hoped to see the play
presented as a warning to Scandinavia not to be drawn into
what became the Second World War, events overtook him,
and the play was not staged until 19 April 1941 in Zurich,
with Therese Giehse as Mother Courage, and with music by
Paul Burkhard. Brecht himself was meanwhile still in
Finland.

Partly as a result of what he had heard of the reaction to
that performance, Brecht made certain changes before he
himself produced the play at the Deutsches Theater in Berlin
in 1949, with Helene Weigel now in the lead. His aim was to
avoid the dangers of sentimentality in the central role. The
music was now by Paul Dessau. Other important changes in
the text and in the ordering of the events were suggested by
the actors.

The English premiere was in Barnstaple, Devon, in 1955
with Joan Littlewood playing Mother Courage in her own
production. Jerome Robbins directed the play on Broadway
in 1963 with Anne Bancroft in the title role.

As part of their aim of encouraging standard productions,
the Berliner Ensemble published a photographic model-book,
as Brecht put it, 'not to render thought unnecessary, but to
provoke it.' It was on this model-book that William Gaskill
based the first National Theatre production of the play with
Madge Ryan at the Old Vic in 1965.

D.H.

Mother Courage and Her Children

This version of *Mother Courage and her Children* was first
performed in the Olivier auditorium of the National Theatre
on 3 November 1995. The cast was as follows:

Characters

Anna Fierling, Mother Courage	Diana Rigg
Kattrin, *her dumb daughter*	Lesley Sharp
Eilif, *her elder son*	Brett Fancy
Swiss.Cheese, *her younger son*	Bohdan Poraj
The Cook	Geoffrey Hutchings
The Chaplain	David Bradley
Yvette Pottier	Doon Mackichan
The Recruiting Officer	John Bluthal
The Sergeant	Tony Selby
The Commander-in-Chief	Donald Pickering
The Armourer	Gordon Langford-Rowe
A Soldier	Ken Christiansen
The Second Sergeant	Anthony Renshaw
The Man with a Patch	Paul Benzing
A Very Old Colonel	Michael Gough
Two Mercenaries	James Buller
	Ken Christiansen
The Regimental Clerk	Cyril Shaps
Young Soldier	Patrick Baladi
Older Soldier	Gordon Langford-Rowe
Soldier in Fur Coat	Angus Wright
Second Soldier	Anthony Renshaw
Farmer's Wife	Phillipa Peak
A Peasant	Paul Benzing
The Soldier in the Bar	James Buller
Young Man	Martin Freeman
Old Woman	Sarah Parks
Eilif's Guards	Patrick Baladi
	Ken Christiansen
	Anthony Renshaw
The Singer	Tamsin Dives

Lieutenant	Angus Wright
First Soldier	Patrick Baladi
Second Soldier	James Buller
Third Soldier	Anthony Renshaw
Peasant in Halle	Edward Clayton
Peasant's Son	Ken Christiansen
Peasant's Wife	Susan Jane Tanner

Directed by Jonathan Kent
Designed by Paul Bond
Lighting by Peter Mumford
Music by Jonathan Dove
Original translation by Anthony Meech

Setting

The play is set between 1624 and 1636, during two wars: the Polish-Swedish War and the Thirty Years War.

In Brecht's own production an interval was taken, as here, after Scene Seven.

1 Sweden. 1624.

A country road near a town in Dalecaria. The Swedish Commander-in-Chief is raising troops for the campaign in Poland. To this end, a **Recruiting Officer** *and a* **Sergeant** *stand shivering in the freezing cold.*

Recruiting Officer How can anyone raise an army in a place like this? Sweden! I'm seriously thinking of killing myself. By the twelfth of next month I've got to get four units together. God knows how. When I do finally get hold of a possible and sort of ignore the pigeon chest and the varicose veins, I've no sooner got him blind drunk and signing on the dotted line than I turn to pay for the brandy, and wham! he's out the lavatory window. I tell you, there's no such thing as honour any more. Pride. Duty. What do they mean? I'm losing my faith in the human race.

Sergeant Well, that's the problem, isn't it? They haven't had a war here for such a long time. Without a good war, where do you get your moral standards from? Everything goes to pot in peacetime. People eat what they like. You see them wandering about with cheese on their bread and then a great smear of bacon fat on top! How many men are there in that town down the road? How many horses? Nobody knows. They've never even been counted. I've been in places where they haven't had a war for seventy years. People can't even remember their own names. They can't tell each other apart. It's only when war comes you get proper lists. Everything numbered and with a label round its neck. It's obvious. No war. No order.

Recruiting Officer It's true.

Sergeant Of course, as with all good things, it's hard to get a proper war started. Once it starts, of course, there's no stopping it, thank God. But at the beginning . . . well, people are always frightened of the new.

At once music is heard. A canteen cart is pulled on by two young men. Sitting on it are **Mother Courage**, *playing a mouth organ, and her dumb daughter,* **Kattrin**. *The* **Sergeant** *goes out to stop the cart.*

Recruiting Officer   Hold on, what've we got here? Two
tarts and two possibles, by the look of it.

She begins to sing.

Mother Courage
   Nobody goes to war without good shoes to wear
   Mother Courage comes with boots to fit your feet
   Take off those slabs of dirty cardboard
   Untie those filthy, ragged strips of sheet
   Your commanders want you springing into battle
   They hardly want you limping into town
   Come on, they want to see you fit and smiling
   As you march towards the guns that mow you down

     Spring is here. The snows are melting
     The dead are gone. They're all at peace
     And what remains must now continue
     That's us. Let's go. We're all that's left.

The **Recruiting Officer** *has been hovering round these promising
arrivals.*

Recruiting Officer   I tell you, if this doesn't work I'm
finished. I'm not stopping here till the middle of April . . .

Mother Courage
   Commanders, give your men their rations
   Why not eat and drink with them as well
   Then when they're full
   When they're standing ready
   Please, you have my blessing
   Send them cheerful to the gaping jaws of hell.

     Spring is here. The snows are melting
     The dead are gone. They're all at peace
     And what remains must now continue
     That's us. Let's go. We're all that's left.

Sergeant   Right. What do you do?

Mother Courage   We are in business.

Sergeant   Who are you with?

Eilif   The Second Regiment.

Sergeant   Papers.

Mother Courage *has already got a roll of papers out of a tin box and is climbing down from her cart.*

Mother Courage   Here we are, every paper I've got. Look, some pages of the Bible. Great for wrapping gherkins in. This is a road-map of Moravia. Never been there, I think I might throw that one away. This . . . now this is a beautiful certificate, signed and sealed, proving my horse hasn't got foot-and-mouth disease. Unfortunately, he is however dead. Cost two hundred shillings. I didn't pay, thank God. Is that enough paper for you?

Sergeant   Spare us the cabaret. You need a licence.

Swiss Cheese   A licence?

Mother Courage   My face is my licence.

Swiss Cheese   This is Mother Courage!

Sergeant   Never heard of her.

Mother Courage   Honesty written all over it.

Sergeant   Courage? What kind of name is that?

Mother Courage   I was once so scared of going bust I drove my cart right through the bombardment of Riga – right through the heart of it – with fifty loaves of bread in the back. That's why they call me Courage. Mind you, the bread was going mouldy, I didn't have much choice.

Recruiting Officer   Sergeant, I think she's winding you up.

Mother Courage   Wind him up? In front of my innocent children?

Recruiting Officer I'd say we've got a subversive. What the army requires is discipline.

Mother Courage I thought what the army required was sausage.

Sergeant Name.

Mother Courage Anna Fierling.

The **Sergeant** *starts to write.*

Sergeant So you're all called Fierling?

Mother Courage Certainly not.

Sergeant I thought you said they were your children.

Mother Courage That doesn't mean they've all got to have the same name.

Sergeant What, all different?

Mother Courage You're not saying you've never come across that before?

She points at **Eilif**.

His dad was a soldier. Like you. Only cleverer. And the boy never met him. I was with a Frenchman by the time he was born.

The **Sergeant** *points at the younger son.*

Sergeant So I suppose this one's Chinese?

Mother Courage Swiss, since you ask. Only by then I was with a Hungarian. Very nice man as it happened. His kidneys gave out and it wasn't drink either. The boy takes after him.

Sergeant But he wasn't his father?

Mother Courage   No, but he takes after him. We call him Swiss Cheese.

He points to her daughter.

Sergeant   And this one?

Mother Courage   Kattrin Haupt. Half-German.

Sergeant   The extended family!

Mother Courage   Precisely.

He is writing in a book.

Sergeant   And you're from Bamberg in Bavaria. What are you doing here?

Mother Courage   Well, there's no war in Bamberg, is there?

Recruiting Officer (*to* **Eilif**)   Pulling that cart, what are you, dumb bloody animals? They should call you the Ox brothers.

Eilif   Ma, can I hit him? Can I just hit the bastard right now?

Mother Courage   Certainly not. Now, gentlemen, let's see what we can do for you. What do you need? A gun? A nice new buckle for your belt?

Sergeant   No. We need something else. These sons of yours . . .

Mother Courage   Yes?

Sergeant   Built like gods. Barrel-chested.

Mother Courage (*at once*)   No, no, no, you're not having them. No son of mine is going to the war.

Sergeant   Why not? There's money in it and glory as well. Selling shoes is women's work.

He turns to **Eilif**.

Come here, let me see if that's muscle or chicken fat.

Mother Courage It's chicken fat. Give him a look and he keels over.

Recruiting Officer He just insulted me. He called me a bastard. We're going into that field to settle it.

Eilif Please let me, Ma. I can take him apart.

Mother Courage Leave him! You're not having him! This boy is a killer, I warn you. A killer! He carries a knife in his boot.

Recruiting Officer Does he really? I look forward to that. (*To* **Eilif**.) Come on, let's do it!

Mother Courage He's just a boy. He's a child. You'll get your five shillings for finding him, and all he'll get is a bullet in the neck.

She draws a knife herself.

Try it and I'll kill you myself. This is a respectable business. We're just making a living.

Sergeant Respectable? With a knife in your hand, I hardly think so, you old witch. Put your knife away. Come on, you're doing very nicely out of this war. How's it to go on with no soldiers?

Mother Courage Yeah, but they don't have to be mine.

Sergeant Ah I see, right. The war's there for what you get out of it, eh? Not sure why they call you Courage. When you're frightened of the war.

Eilif I'm not frightened of anything.

Sergeant I'm sure. Why should you be? Look at me. I joined up at seventeen.

Mother Courage Oh yeah? And how long d'you think you'll last?

Sergeant What are you saying? I'm not going to make it?

Mother Courage I know you're not. I only need to look at you.

Swiss Cheese   Psychic, you see. She's got the gift, my mum. Everyone says.

Recruiting Officer   Oh really? Then go on, do the Sergeant.

Sergeant   I don't believe in that stuff.

Mother Courage   Don't you? Give me your helmet.

He gives it to her.

Sergeant   I'm just doing this for a laugh. I'm not that stupid.

Mother Courage *takes a piece of parchment and starts to tear it into pieces.*

Mother Courage   Just for you, just this once, I'm doing it for free. I put a big black cross on one of these slips. Black is death.

Swiss Cheese   She leaves the other ones blank, you see?

Mother Courage   I fold them, I put them in the helmet, I mix them up. Just as mankind is mixed together, from the moment of our birth. Now choose.

As the **Sergeant** *hesitates, the* **Recruiting Officer** *is still working on* **Eilif**.

Recruiting Officer   I promise you I don't just take anyone. I need a man's man. Who eats red meat and knows how to enjoy himself.

Sergeant (*fishing in the helmet*)   It means nothing! It's meaningless!

Swiss Cheese   He's got the black cross! He's going to die!

Recruiting Officer   Take no notice, they're having you on.

Sergeant (*hoarse*)   It's a fiddle. You've cheated me.

Mother Courage   No. You cheated yourself the day you joined the army. So now let's be going. We need to get moving, there isn't a war every day of the week.

Sergeant   I'm not fooled by this. We're taking your son and that's it.

Eilif   I want to do it, Ma. I really want to join up.

Mother Courage   Who asked you, you stupid Finn?

Eilif   Ask Swiss Cheese. He wants to as well.

Mother Courage   Really? It's the first I've heard of it. All right, I can see I'm going to have to do the three of you as well.

She goes away upstage to draw crosses on more slips. The **Recruiting Officer** *persists with* **Eilif**.

Recruiting Officer   Don't believe all that stuff about how you have to pray if you're in the Swedish Army. It's a libel, all right? We do have a quick hymn on Sundays, but you can just mime it, nobody minds.

Mother Courage *returns with the slips which she drops into the* **Sergeant**'s *helmet. She holds the helmet out to* **Eilif**.

Mother Courage   Dip. Confront your destiny.

Eilif *fishes in the helmet and unfolds it. She grabs it from him.*

Mother Courage   Oh, no, I don't believe it. The plight of motherhood is a terrible thing. To be cut down in the springtime of his life! Here. It is written. Listen to what fate is telling you. If you become a soldier, you will die. (*Shouts at him.*) Is that what you want?

Eilif   Of course not. No! I mean, *no!*

Recruiting Officer   All right, if this one's bottling out, I'll take the brother.

Mother Courage   Ah well then, we'd better do him as well. Come on. You'll be all right. You're honest.

Swiss Cheese *fishes in the helmet.*

Mother Courage   No, surely, please, no surely not. Your eyes. You are looking strangely. Surely, not another child of mine.

She takes the slip.

Sergeant, tell me what this is? Do I see black?

Sergeant (*angry*)   Yes. Yes, it's bloody black.

He turns to the **Recruiting Officer**.

It can't be a fiddle. Her own children get them as well.

Mother Courage *is moving across to* **Kattrin**.

Mother Courage   All right then, you, my darling daughter, you at least I am sure of. You have a good heart.

She holds the helmet up to her on the cart but takes the slip out herself.

Oh, this is too strange. Your very kindness will lead you to your death. Take heed, daughter. Lie low and stay silent. Not that you've much choice in the matter. So now you all know. Every one of you. Every one of you has been warned. On our way, children. It's time to move on.

She gives the **Sergeant** *his helmet back and climbs onto the cart to go.*

Recruiting Officer (*to the* **Sergeant**)   Do something quick.

Sergeant   I can't. I'm not feeling well.

Recruiting Officer   Come on, get some business going.

He speaks up so **Mother Courage** *can hear.*

I think you should look at the buckle, Sergeant. After all, these good people here live by trade. (*To* **Mother Courage**.) He really likes the look of that buckle, you know.

Mother Courage   For you, a shilling. It's worth four times as much.

She climbs down from the cart.

Sergeant   I need to look at it. Here, come on, let's get out of the wind.

Mother Courage   Doesn't seem windy to me.

He goes behind the cart. **Mother Courage** *goes round to join him.*

Sergeant   I suppose it could be worth a shilling. It's silver.

Mother Courage   It's a solid six ounces.

Sergeant   A shilling it is.

Eilif *stands undecided with the* **Recruiting Officer**.

Sergeant   I don't understand how I got a cross. I'm always at the rear. Sergeant's the safest job there is. You push up the others up front, so they can get the glory. You've quite ruined my lunch, I tell you.

Mother Courage   My advice to you is, stay in the back. Here, have a sip of brandy.

She gives him a drink. The **Recruiting Officer** *is holding a shilling out in his fist, and* **Eilif** *follows him off as if in a trance.*

Recruiting Officer   It's ten shillings, money in your pocket and you get to fight for your King. And women? I tell you, one look at the uniform and they're yours. All right? Then fight me, come on, now you can fight me as much as you like.

They go off shadow-boxing. **Kattrin** *jumps down from the cart and starts making hoarse noises.*

Mother Courage   All right, Kattrin, all right. Give us a moment. The Sergeant is still paying.

She bites the coin he has given her.

I don't trust coins, I've been skinned once too often. But this is good. Where's Eilif?

Swiss Cheese   He went with the Recruiting Officer.

Mother Courage *stands quite still.*

Mother Courage You prick. (*Then to* **Kattrin**.) All right, I know, it's not your fault. It's never your fault, you can't speak.

Sergeant That's life. What can you do? Have a drink yourself. You thought you could live off the war, but keep your family out of it, eh?

Mother Courage It's you now, Kattrin. Help your brother.

Kattrin *and* **Swiss Cheese** *put themselves in harness, and start to pull.* **Mother Courage** *walks alongside. The cart moves off. The* **Sergeant** *watches them go. He sings.*

Sergeant
War's a deal. It cuts both ways.
Whoever takes also pays.
Our age brings forth its new idea:
Total war – and total fear.

2   Poland. 1626.

The **Commander-in-Chief**'s *tent, a kitchen beside it. It is pitched outside the fortress of Wallhof. In the background the noise of battle, the thunder of the guns can be heard.* **The Cook** *is in an argument with* **Mother Courage** *who is trying to sell him a chicken.*

The Cook Six shillings for this miserable bird!

Mother Courage Miserable bird? Are you talking about this beautiful fat beast? Your Commander in Chief . . . greedy as hell, nothing to eat and you're telling me he won't pay six shillings for it?

The Cook I can get a dozen for two shillings just round the corner.

Mother Courage Are you out of your head? A bird as good as this? When we're in the middle of a siege? A famine? You might get a rat, sure, if you're lucky. I've heard there's men out in the fields all day chasing rats for their supper. But this giant capon for what? Just five shillings?

The Cook It's not us that's under siege, for Christ's sake. We're the fucking besiegers.

Mother Courage Sieging, being sieged, doesn't make much difference, does it? At least they stocked up in the town before they went in. I hear they're living like kings. But us? Forget it. Remember, I've been out among the peasants. They've nothing.

The Cook Bollocks. They've plenty. They're just hiding it from the army, that's all.

Mother Courage (*triumphantly*) Nothing, I tell you. Nothing. People are ruined. They're eating the earth. I've seen them digging up roots. They boil leather straps, and drink the broth. As God is my witness, that's how it is. And I have a capon, and I'm supposed to give it away for four shillings.

The Cook I said three, not four.

She tries a new tack.

Mother Courage Look, this chicken . . . this chicken is not an ordinary chicken. This chicken was so gifted, I tell you, it used to boil its own eggs as part of the deal. It's true. Omelette, scrambled, the lot. And you're saying four shillings is too much?

The Cook You know what I'm going to do?

He stops peeling carrots, fishes a rotten piece of meat out of the dustbin, then takes it over to the butcher's block where he holds a knife over it.

This is a very fine piece of beef, which I am about to cook. I'm giving you one minute to think.

Mother Courage Go ahead. Cook it. As it's at least a year old.

The Cook This cow was walking about with a smile on its face, only yesterday. I saw it myself.

Mother Courage Then it must have been stinking even when it was alive.

The Cook   I don't care, I'm stewing it five hours if I have to, and then let's see if it smells.

Mother Courage   Yeah, well, I'd use a lot of pepper if I were you.

The **Commander-in-Chief** *comes into the tent with* **Eilif** *and an Army* **Chaplain**. *He is slapping* **Eilif** *on the shoulder. He is overtly affectionate.*

Commander   Now, sir, you are with your Commander. And you shall sit on my right-hand side. For you, sir, are a perfect chivalrous knight and you have done good in God's name, in a Holy War. I will decorate you personally with a gold medallion when we have taken this town. Here we are, come to save the miserable souls of these filthy peasants, and how do they repay us? By hiding their cattle from us. But you taught them a lesson. Hell, you taught them manners, sir. So let's drink this wine, the two of us and both in one go!

They do so.

And none for our Chaplain here. No drink for the bigots, eh? And now, sweet boy, what can we give you for lunch?

Eilif   A little meat, why not?

Commander   Cook! Meat!

The Cook   He always brings guests when we've nothing to eat.

Mother Courage *signals him to be quiet so she can listen.*

Eilif   Killing peasants makes you hungry.

Mother Courage   Sweet Jesus, it's Eilif.

The Cook   Who?

Mother Courage   My boy. My son. It's been two years I haven't seen him. They took him, when we were on the road. He must be doing well if the Commander invites him for a meal. And what are you offering them? The Commander has a guest. An honoured guest. Take my advice, roast chicken for lunch, and no pissing about. Ten shillings it is.

The **Commander** *has sat down with* **Eilif** *and now yells out.*

Commander Cook, you contemptible oaf, meat for our lunch or I'll strike you dead.

The Cook All right, I'll take it. It's blackmail, but I'll take it.

Mother Courage What, you want this miserable bird?

The Cook Yes, it's miserable. And yes, I'm buying it. And for five shillings.

Mother Courage Ten. Market forces. For my own son, nothing is too good.

The Cook *gives her the money.*

The Cook Well at least you can pluck it while I light the fire.

She sits down to pluck the chicken.

Mother Courage His face when he sees me! I can't wait. He's my best boy, my bravest. I have a stupid one, too. Stupid but honest. And a girl. She's nothing. But one thing in her favour: she can't speak.

Back in the tent the **Commander** *is becoming more expansive.*

Commander Drink, come on. My best Falernian. My last two barrels, but they're yours. I have a true believer in my army at last.

He turns to **The Chaplain**.

And this good shepherd can stand and watch, because he preaches, and knows nothing about the real world. So come, sir, tell us your story. Tell us how you dealt with those peasants and captured the twenty cows. I can't wait for them to get here.

Eilif A day or two at most.

Mother Courage   That's my boy, eh? Not bringing the cows till tomorrow, so I can sell my chicken.

Eilif   I tell you, I knew exactly where they were hiding them. In a wood. Waiting to sell them in town. So I let them round the cows up, why not? Let them do the work for me. Then I starved my own men for two days, so their mouths were watering like dogs.

Commander   Brilliant!

Eilif   The rest was easy. The only problem was, the peasants had clubs. There were four of them, pushed me into the briars, knocked the sword from my hand, screamed at me, 'surrender!' I thought my God, this is the end, they're going to skin me alive.

Commander   What did you do?

Eilif   I laughed.

Commander   What?

Eilif   Laughed. I pretended I'd come to do business. 'Twenty shillings is too much,' I said, 'but I will consider fifteeen.' As if I meant it for real. They all started scratching their heads. Perfect chance. I bent down, picked up my sword, and sliced through the lot of them. Necessity the mother of invention, isn't that what they say?

Commander   Is that what they say, preacher man?

The Chaplain   Strictly speaking the phrase is not in the Bible. But our Lord did turn the five loaves into five hundred, so you could say He was working on the same principle. But things were easier then. People had enough to eat, so they didn't mind being told to love their neighbour. Now . . . well, things are different.

Commander   Very different.

He laughs.

All right, you get a drink for that, you old Pharisee.

He turns back to **Eilif**.

You're a good Christian, Eilif. What does it say in the scriptures? 'Whatsoever thou doest for the least of my brethren, thou doest for me.' And what have you done for everyone? You've guaranteed them a proper steak dinner.

Eilif I bent down, I reached for my sword and I sliced them into pieces!

Commander You are a young Caeser, sir. You should be presented to the King.

Eilif I've seen him from a distance. He gives off a kind of glow. I try to model myself on him.

Commander Plainly. You don't know how much it means to me, Eilif, to have a soldier like you under my command. I shall treat you as my son.

He leads him to the map.

Now, come and see how we're placed, we've still a long way to go. There are chances for glory ahead.

Mother Courage *has been listening and now plucks angrily at the chicken.*

Mother Courage He must be a rotten general.

The Cook Hungry, sure. But why rotten?

Mother Courage Because he needs brave soldiers, that's why. If he knew what he was doing, he wouldn't need them to be brave. It's always the same. Whenever heroics are called for, it's a sure sign someone's fucked up.

The Cook I'd have thought the opposite.

Mother Courage Come on, think about it. What's courage? Failure of planning, that's all. Some general takes his troops into some stupid situation. Or he's tried to save money and hired too few of them in the first place. It's sort of a law, isn't it? The stupider and more useless the general, the more exceptional the men need to be. Like it's only a badly-run country where the people have to be special. In a proper country, there's no need of virtue. Everyone can just get on with being so-so. Averagely intelligent. And for all I care, cowards as well.

Commander   I bet your father was a soldier.

Eilif   He was. A great one, I'm told. You should have heard my mother on the subject.

He begins to sing, dancing a war-dance with his sabre.

Commander (*yelling out*)   Where's the bloody food?

Eilif
   A woman said goodbye to a soldier
   She held him and kissed him one day
   She looked at his knife and his gun at the bedside
   And implored him to throw them away
   He just laughed at the very suggestion
   She said 'It's not the gun, it's the danger it brings
   For a man who carries a pistol ignores
   The danger of much more dangerous things.'

     Oh beware, beware, beware
     Those who hear this
     The advice that the soldier received
     For the rest of his life he remembered the woman
     The woman he should have believed

   He took her to one side and he laughed at her
   He told her he could catch the knife with his hands
   She begged him 'Please at least fear the water'
   He just smiled and said his heart was a man's
   She said 'I will stand and watch on the roof for you
   The silver moon will be out I will wait
   And when you're in danger I beg you remember
   You could have avoided your fate.'

In the kitchen **Mother Courage** *takes up the song, hitting a pot with a spoon.*

Mother Courage
   Oh beware, beware, beware
   Those who hear this

The advice that the soldier received
For the rest of his life he remembered the woman
The woman he should have believed.

Eilif   Who's that?

Mother Courage
So the soldier reached the river at midnight
As he tried to cross the rapids he fell
He drowned in the fast-flowing water
And the knife and the gun sank as well
The woman on the roof, she stood waiting
The moon shone down on her long flowing hair
Oh the moon! Oh the woman still standing!
The dead soldier who did not beware!

Oh beware, beware, beware!
Those who hear this
The advice that the soldier received
For just as he died he remembered the woman
The woman he should have believed.

Commander   Really, it's always the kitchen staff.

Eilif *has gone into the kitchen and is embracing his mother.*

Eilif   My God, I can't believe it! Where are the others?
How are they?

She is in his arms.

Mother Courage   Happy as pigs in mud. Swiss Cheese is
Paymaster to the Second Regiment. I couldn't keep him out
the war altogether, but at least he won't be in the action.

Eilif   How are your feet, Ma?

Mother Courage   Murder in the morning, getting into my
boots.

The **Commander** *has joined them.*

Commander   So you're his mother? I hope you can give me more sons like this.

Eilif   So you heard me being honoured for my deeds.

Mother Courage   Yes I heard.

She starts boxing his ears. He covers his cheek.

Eilif   Hey, what's that for? Because I stole cattle?

Mother Courage   It's for fighting back. Why didn't you surrender when the four men attacked you? You dumb Finnish idiot. Have I taught you nothing?

3   Poland. 1629.

A military camp in Poland, the regimental flag flying on a pole.
Mother Courage *has stretched a washing line from a large cannon to the cart which is now laden with all kinds of goods. She is folding washing on the cannon with* **Kattrin**, *while at the same time bartering with an* **Armourer** *for a sack of bullets.* **Swiss Cheese** *is looking on, now in the uniform of Finnish Paymaster.*

An attractive young woman, **Yvette Pottier**, *is sewing a beautiful hat. She has a glass of brandy beside her. She is in her stockinged feet, a pair of high-heeled red boots just to one side.*

Armourer   You can have the bullets for two shillings. Dirt cheap. It's an emergency. The colonel's been on the booze with his officers for two days and the drink's run out.

Mother Courage   These are army property. If I'm caught with them I'll be court-martialled. You sell them and your poor bloody soldiers will have nothing to shoot with.

Armourer   Oh spare me, please. This is business.

Mother Courage   I'm not taking Army Goods. Not at that price.

Armourer   You buy them from me at two, tonight you sell at five, even eight, to the Fourth Regiment's Armourer. And you give him a phoney receipt for twelve. I know for a fact he's clean out of ammunition.

Mother Courage Then why not do it yourself?

Armourer I don't trust him. He's a friend.

Mother Courage *takes the sack.*

Mother Courage Give it here.

She turns to **Kattrin**.

Take him round the back and give him a shilling and a half.

The Armourer *protests.*

I said, a shilling and a half.

Kattrin *drags the sack round the back, the* **Armourer** *following her.* **Mother Courage** *addresses* **Swiss Cheese**.

Mother Courage Here, take your winter woollies, and look after them. It's October, and there's a fair chance winter's coming. I say fair chance, because the one thing I've learnt is that nothing is certain except that nothing is certain. Not even the seasons. Though you do have to make your regimental accounts add up. Do they add up?

Swiss Cheese Yes, Ma.

Mother Courage Never forget, they made you paymaster because you were honest, not a chancer like your brother, and most of all because you're so stupid you'll never even think of running away with the money. That's a great comfort to me. And don't lose the long johns.

Swiss Cheese No, Ma. They're going under my mattress.

He begins to go, when the **Armourer** *calls to him.*

Armourer I'll walk with you, Paymaster.

Mother Courage Don't teach him any of your tricks on the way!

The **Armourer** *leaves with* **Swiss Cheese** *without saying goodbye.*
Yvette *waves.*

Yvette   He might at least say goodbye.

Mother Courage   I don't like to see them together. He's not
a good influence. But at least the war's going well. Box
clever, do nothing stupid and business'll be fine. I don't
think you should be drinking with your present complaint.

Yvette   Who says I've got a complaint?

Mother Courage   I think more or less everyone does.

Yvette   It's a bloody lie! Courage, I'm desperate. No one'll
come near me. They go right past me like I'm an open drain.

She suddenly throws her hat away in anger.

Oh, what's the point? What's the point of trying to look nice?
That's why I'm drinking. I never did before. It puts lines on
your face, but what the hell? What difference does it make?
Every soldier for miles around knows what I look like
underneath. I should have stayed at home when the first
man betrayed me. Pointless being proud. Eat shit, or down
you go.

Mother Courage   Oh, not the Pieter story again and how it
all started. Spare us. Not in front of my poor innocent
daughter.

Yvette   She's the one who should hear it. Harden her
against love.

Mother Courage   No one's ever hardened against love.

Music begins to play.

Yvette   I tell you, I grew up in Flanders, beautiful Flanders'
fields, that's where it started. Otherwise, we'd never have
met, and I wouldn't be sitting here now in Poland. He was
an army cook, fair-haired, a Dutchman, but skinny. You'll
soon find out, Kattrin: the skinny ones are the worst. I didn't
even know he had another girl at the time. She called him

Piet the Pipe, because he kept his pipe in his mouth, even
while he was doing it, it meant that little to him . . .

I was just a girl of seventeen
When the army came to town
The invaders put aside their swords
And laid their muskets down

Each night in May
The drums would sound
The flag come down
The army stand
And then at dusk they all lay down . . .
. . . and fraternised

I was young, this soldier came
He took my heart on sight
I learned that what you hate by day
You come to love at night

Each night in May
The drums would sound
The flag come down
The army stand
And then at dusk they all lay down . . .
. . . and fraternised

The love
The love
The love I felt
Had a power that came from above
To this day I feel that power
The heavenly power of love

But then in May
The drums did sound
The flag came down
The army stood
And then at dusk they all left town . . .
. . . and vanished.

The sad thing is, I followed him, but I never found him again. And that was many years ago.

She walks unsteadily behind the cart.

Mother Courage   Don't forget your hat.

Yvette   Whoever wants it can have it.

Mother Courage   Let that be a lesson to you, Kattrin. Have nothing to do with the military. You heard her, love's a heavenly power. Even if he's not in the army. At the best of times, it's not easy. He says he wants to kiss the ground you walk on, and suddenly it's not him on the ground, it's you, flat on your back and a slave for life. Just be thankful you're dumb. You can't say one thing today, and another the next. Or want to bite your tongue off because you told the truth. Being dumb's a great gift from God.

The Cook *and* **The Chaplain** *come on.*

Mother Courage   So now it's the Cook, what's he want?

The Chaplain   I've come with a message for you from your son, Eilif. And the Cook came along because you've made such a profound impression on him.

The Cook   I just wanted some air.

Mother Courage   You can have some of our air, as long as you behave decently, and even if you don't I think I can handle it. What does Eilif want? I've got no money.

The Chaplain   Actually it's a request to his brother, the Paymaster.

Mother Courage   He's gone, he's not here. And I'm not having Eilif leading the poor boy into wickedness.

She takes money out of the purse which is slung round her neck.

Here, let him have some of mine. He should be ashamed of himself, exploiting a mother's love.

The Cook   Oh come on, for fuck's sake, give him more than that. His regiment's on the move and he's off, maybe to his death. Mothers always say 'oh I won't spoil the kid', then later they're sorry. Once he's dead, you can't dig him up.

The Chaplain All right, Cook, it's all very well to be cynical. But this war happens to be a little different. To die in this war is a blessing, not an inconvenience. This is a war of faith.

The Cook Oh yes, you're right, no question. I mean, on the surface it may look like an ordinary war, there's all the usual features, looting and killing and plundering and so on. You even come across an occasional rape. But don't let that fool you: it's a religious war.

The Chaplain *turns to* **Mother Courage**, *gesturing towards* **The Cook**.

The Chaplain I did try to stop him coming, but he says you've got to him. He dreams of you at night.

The Cook *is lighting his pipe*.

The Cook I wanted a glass of brandy from a woman's hand. Even a religious war can make you thirsty. What's wrong with that? (*To* **The Chaplain**.) You're in no position to disapprove. The stories you were telling me as we walked over . . .

Mother Courage And you a man of the cloth. I think I'd better get you a drink, or you'll both be talking dirty at me out of sheer boredom.

The Chaplain Temptation, said the preacher, and at once gave way.

As they go, he turns towards **Kattrin**.

And who is this delightful young person?

Mother Courage That person is not delightful. She's my daughter.

The Chaplain *and* **The Cook** *go behind the cart with* **Mother Courage**. *They can be heard talking politics from the other side but we watch* **Kattrin** *as she leaves her washing and crosses to the discarded hat.*

Mother Courage   Mind you, I don't know what we're
doing in Poland in the first place. I blame the Poles. I know
it was our King who invaded their country, but – be fair – he
was just about to pull out when suddenly they started
wanting to run their own affairs, and decided to attack him.
Anything that's coming to them now, seems to me is their
own fault.

The Chaplain   The King's only interest is freedom. It's the
Kaiser who enslaved them, Poles and Germans alike. Our
King had no choice. He had to set them free.

The Cook   Ah, how very true, my own view exactly. I knew
the brandy'd be good here.

Kattrin *has picked up the hat and is now drawing the red boots
towards her.*

The Cook   Oh, it's been a nightmare for the poor bloody
King, no question. First he had to introduce the salt tax in
Sweden to pay for the war. So he's bankrupted all his
subjects. Not that he lets that get him down, of course. Then
he comes here to Poland to give them their freedom. Then
when he moves on and tries to give the Germans their
freedom, there's a whole lot of them who'd rather not have it,
thank you, so he has to string them up and cut their
stomachs out and so on. So here he is getting nothing for all
his efforts and kindness. But he does have one thing in his
favour. He's doing it all for God, which is a mercy, because
otherwise people might say he was doing it for the money.
But as it's God he's doing it for, his conscience is clear, and
after all, that's the main thing.

Mother Courage   I can tell you're not Swedish, or you
wouldn't speak of the Great Hero King in that way.

The Chaplain   I might remind you, you eat his bread.

The Cook   I bake it. He eats it.

Mother Courage   To hear them all talk, you'd think these
people at the top waged war for the fear of God and in the
name of everything that's fine and noble. But just look into

it, you'll find they're not that stupid. They're fighting for money. And just as well. Otherwise the little people like you and me wouldn't bother to join in.

The Cook Exactly.

The Chaplain I think as a Dutchman you'd do well to look at the flag above you before you express an opinion about a war in Poland.

Mother Courage Oh we're all good Protestants here.

The Cook Cheers!

Kattrin *has put on* **Yvette**'s *hat and begun strutting about, imitating her way of walking. But suddenly there is the sound of cannon fire and guns. Drums sound.* **Mother Courage**, **The Cook** *and* **The Chaplain** *come running out from behind the cart, the men still holding their drinks. The* **Armourer** *and a* **Soldier** *run to the cannon and try to start moving it.*

Mother Courage Hang on, I've got my washing on that.

She tries to save it.

Armourer Surprise attack. It's the Catholics. I think we may be too late. (*To the* **Soldier**.) Get that gun out of here.

He rushes off.

The Cook Shit, I must get back to my Commander. I'll come by for another chat in a day or two.

Mother Courage *shouts at his departing figure.*

Mother Courage Hold on, you've forgotten your pipe!

The Cook Keep it for me. I'll be needing it.

Mother Courage Of course this has to happen, just when business is looking up.

The Chaplain I'd better go too. It could get dangerous. Blessed are the peacemakers, that's what they say. But I really need a coat.

Mother Courage   I don't lend coats, even when it's life or death. I've had some bad times lending coats.

The Chaplain   I'm very conspicuous.

She hands him a coat.

Mother Courage   I'm doing this against my better judgement. Now get out of here.

The Chaplain   Thank you, that's kind. But if you don't mind I think I'm safer just sitting down here. If I run I may attract enemy fire.

Mother Courage *shouts at the* **Soldier**.

Mother Courage   Leave it, you idiot, no one's paying you for that. I'll look after it, if you don't want to die.

Soldier (*running away*)   You're my witness. I did try my best.

Mother Courage   Yeah, I'll testify.

She sees **Kattrin** *in the hat.*

What the hell are you doing, dressed up like a whore? Have you gone crazy?

She tears it off **Kattrin**'s *head.*

And, oh Christ, just look at the shoes.

She starts trying to tug at the boots, then gestures towards **The Chaplain**.

Sweet Jesus, Chaplain, give me a hand. I'll be back in a sec.

She runs off to the cart as **Yvette** *arrives powdering herself.*

Yvette   I've just heard. There's Catholics arriving. Where's my hat for God's sake? I've got to look decent if the Catholics are here. What on earth will they think? I haven't got a mirror. (*To* **The Chaplain**.) What do you think? Too much powder?

The Chaplain   Well, I'd say, er looks pretty good.

Yvette   And where are my boots?

Kattrin *at once tucks her feet under her skirt to hide them.*

Yvette   I know I left them here. Oh shit, I'll go barefoot. Christ, what you have to endure!

She goes out. **Swiss Cheese** *comes running on carrying a cash box, as* **Mother Courage** *returns with handfuls of ashes which she shows to* **Kattrin**.

Mother Courage   Ashes!

Then she turns to **Swiss Cheese**.

What have you got there?

Swiss Cheese   The regimental cash box.

Mother Courage   For God's sake throw it away. Forget being a paymaster!

Swiss Cheese   But it's my job!

He goes to the back of the cart. **Mother Courage** *starts rubbing ashes into* **Kattrin**'*s face as she addresses* **The Chaplain**.

Mother Courage   Get your cassock off, Chaplain, or that coat's no use to you. (*To* **Kattrin**.) Hold still. Put some muck on your face and you'll be all right. What a shambles! Usual thing, they're saying the sentries were drunk. Hide your light under a bushel, my darling. We all know what Catholics are like. They see a girl with a clean face and five mintues later there's one more whore in the world. Yeah, that's good. You look really dirty. Like you've been rolling in muck. Stop trembling. Nothing's going to happen with you looking like that.

She turns to **Swiss Cheese**.

Where did you put the cash box?

Swiss Cheese   I hid it on the cart.

Mother Courage   Christ Almighty, I do not believe it. If I just turn away, even for a minute! You'd have us all killed.

Swiss Cheese   I'll put it somewhere else. I'll run away with it.

Mother Courage   No, stay here. It's too late.

The Chaplain *is half-changed, downstage.*

The Chaplain   For goodness' sake, the flag!

At once, **Mother Courage** *starts hauling it down.*

Mother Courage   Bugger me, I didn't notice. This one's been up for twenty-five years.

The thunder of the cannons grows louder.

Three days later. Morning. The first meal in the Catholic camp. The cannon has gone. **Mother Courage**, **Kattrin**, **Swiss Cheese** and **The Chaplain** *are sitting eating gloomily together,* **Swiss Cheese** *slightly to one side because he wants to get away.*

Swiss Cheese   Three days we've been here, doing nothing. I know, I just know what the Sergeant's saying. He's bound to be asking 'Where the hell is Swiss Cheese? And where is that box?'

Mother Courage   Just be grateful. They've no idea where you are.

The Chaplain   What about me? This is no life. I can't even hold a service. My heart is overflowing, I am aching to speak of what is in me, but it's as if my tongue has been cut out.

Mother Courage   I've got one on either side. One with his faith, the other with his cash box. I don't know which is more dangerous.

The Chaplain   We are all in God's hands.

Mother Courage   Oh I wouldn't say things were as bad as that. Though I must say I am having a bit of trouble sleeping. It's Swiss Cheese that worries me. For myself, I think I did pretty well. Half-way through the interrogation I broke into a few Hail Marys, and offered them communion candles at half-price. I'd say they were fooled. I've got the language off pat because Swiss Cheese's dad was a Catholic. Of a kind. What they really wanted was a canteen for the regiment, so perhaps they weren't fooled and they're just turning a blind eye. It hardly matters. We're prisoners, but so are fleas on a dog's back.

The Chaplain It's good milk. But I fear we shall have to start cutting back. After all, we have been defeated.

Mother Courage Who's been defeated? Not me. Defeat for the generals is nothing to do with us. Defeat can be quite nice for people at the bottom. What's that? Honour! What's that? One battle we lost, I got a big white horse out of it. It pulled my cart for seven months before they checked up. No, as a rule I'd say for us at the bottom there's not much difference between victory and defeat. Best times for us are when politics gets bogged down solid.

She turns to **Swiss Cheese**.

Eat!

Swiss Cheese I can't. I'm frightened. How's the Sergeant going to pay the wages?

Mother Courage You don't have pay-day on a retreat.

Swiss Cheese But they won't retreat, will they? If they don't get paid? They're going to refuse. After all, that's their right.

Mother Courage You know, Swiss Cheese, the truth is, I'm slightly in awe of you. I mean, I know I brought you up to be honest, because you've got no brains, but even so, there are limits. And now I'm going to take the Chaplain off to buy a Catholic flag. Look for some meat, as well. There's no one better than the Chaplain at finding meat. It's like he divines it. His mouth starts watering at fifty paces. Thank God we're still trading. The great mercy is, you don't ask a businessman what he believes in. You just ask him 'How much?'

She disappears into the cart.

The Chaplain She's still worried about the cash box.
We've got away with it so far. They think we all work on the
cart. But for how long?

Swiss Cheese I can throw it away.

The Chaplain I'm not sure. That might be more
dangerous. There are spies everywhere. Yesterday I was
relieving myself in a ditch when one popped up right in front
of me. This spy was horrible. A sort of runt with a patch
over one eye. Like a cyclops. I was so scared I nearly let out
a spontaneous prayer. I'm told they now detect Protestants
by smelling their excrement.

Mother Courage *clambers out of the cart with a basket.*

Mother Courage What the hell are these? You slut!

Triumphantly she lifts up the red boots.

Yvette's red boots! Stolen! She's shameless! All because you
went and told her she was delightful!

She puts them back in the basket.

I mean, at least Yvette does it for money, that's one thing,
but *you* . . . if I didn't stop you, you'd do it for fun. How
many times have I told you? Not till the war is over. No
soldiers, under any circumstances. You're not to flaunt
yourself till peace comes.

The Chaplain She doesn't flaunt herself.

Mother Courage Enough. She flaunts herself enough. As
far as I'm concerned I'll only be happy when people say 'I
never noticed her. She wasn't even there. She was just one
more brick in the wall.'

She turns to **Swiss Cheese**.

Leave that box where it is, don't touch it. And keep an eye
on your sister, God knows she needs it. Between the two of
you . . . I'd rather try and keep maggots in a drawer.

She goes out with **The Chaplain**. **Kattrin** *starts to clear the dishes away.*

Swiss Cheese Won't be many more days you can sit out in your shirtsleeves.

Kattrin *points at a tree.*

Swiss Cheese That's right. The leaves are turning yellow.

Kattrin *gestures to ask him something.*

Swiss Cheese No. No drink, thank you. I've got to think.

There's a pause.

I don't know, if Ma can't sleep, maybe it's best I get rid of the box. All right, I will have a drink.

Kattrin *goes behind the cart.*

Swiss Cheese I'm going to put it in that rat hole by the river. Then tonight maybe I'll take it to the regiment. It can't take that long to catch up. It'll really shock the Sergeant. He'll say 'Swiss Cheese, I'm pleasantly disappointed. I put you in charge of the cash box, and all you do is bring it back.'

Kattrin *reappears from behind the cart with a glass of brandy in her hand. Two men confront her, one a* **Sergeant**, *the other the* **Man with a Patch** *over one eye.*

Patch Good morning, miss. I'm wondering if you've seen anyone from the Second Regiment?

Terrified, **Kattrin** *runs downstage, spilling the brandy. The two men look at each other, then seeing* **Swiss Cheese** *they withdraw.* **Swiss Cheese** *is woken from his thoughts.*

Swiss Cheese Look, you're spilling it. What are the faces for? What have you done? Poked yourself in the eye? I'm going to go. I've decided it's the best thing to do.

He gets up. He ignores her frantic attempts to make him understand the danger.

Sweet one, I wish I understood you. I know you mean well.
Don't worry about the brandy, I promise you, there's no
need to be so upset. I'll drink many more brandies in my life.

He takes the box from the cart and hides it under his jacket.

I'll be right back. Now let me go or I'll get angry. I know.
Oh, I wish you could talk.

*He kisses her as she tries to hold him back, then he tears himself away
and goes out. She becomes desperate, running backwards and forwards,
letting out little sounds. As **The Chaplain** and **Mother Courage**
return, she rushes over to her mother.*

Mother Courage   What's this? What's happening? Come
on, tell me. Have they touched you? Where's Swiss Cheese?
Slow down. Step by step. Explain. He took the box? I'll kill
him, the little shit. Take it slow, don't gabble, use your
hands. When you howl, it's very unattractive. What will the
Chaplain think?

Kattrin *at once modifies her manner.*

Mother Courage   What? A man with one eye was here?

The Chaplain   He's the spy. Have they taken Swiss
Cheese?

Kattrin *shakes her head, shrugs her shoulders.*

The Chaplain   We're finished.

Mother Courage *has taken a Catholic flag from the basket and is
now giving it to* **The Chaplain** *to fix to the pole.*

Mother Courage   Put out the new flag.

The Chaplain (*bitter*)   Oh we're all good Catholics here.

Voices are heard. The two men are bringing in **Swiss Cheese**. *As
always* **Mother Courage** *carries on working.*

Swiss Cheese   Let me go. I've got nothing on me. You're
breaking my arm. I'm innocent.

Sergeant   He came from over here. These are his friends.

Mother Courage   Friends? Us?

Swiss Cheese   I don't know who she is. I've never seen her before. I just bought my lunch here. That's why you saw me here. It cost a shilling. And it was salty.

Sergeant   Who are you people?

Mother Courage   We're respectable. We're in business. He bought his lunch here, it's true. He complained it was salty, that's right.

Sergeant   You're trying to pretend you don't know him.

Mother Courage   I don't know any of them. I don't ask them their names. Or if they're heretics. If they pay, then they're not heretics. Are you a heretic?

Swiss Cheese   Of course not.

The Chaplain   He was fine. Really. He sat there. He never opened his mouth. Except to eat. I mean, then he had to.

Sergeant   Who are you?

Mother Courage   Him? He's the barman. He'll get you some brandy. You must be exhausted.

Sergeant   No drinking on duty. (*To* **Swiss Cheese**.) You had something under your shirt, I saw it. You hid it by the river.

Mother Courage   Are you sure you got the right man?

Swiss Cheese   It was another man. I saw him. It was another man with something under his shirt.

Mother Courage   This happens all the time. It's a problem. People make these mistakes. I tell you, I know about these things. I'm Mother Courage, everyone's heard of me. Ask. I'm a great judge of character, and this one . . . I tell you, this one is honest.

Sergeant   It's the regimental cash box we're after. And we know what the man looks like. It's you.

Swiss Cheese   It isn't!

Sergeant   You tell us, or that's it. Where is it?

Mother Courage (*urgently*)   For God's sake, he'd say if he knew. He's not that stupid. He'd say, look, here you are, here it is. That's what he'd say. Come on, you idiot, the Sergeant's giving you a chance.

Swiss Cheese   What if I haven't got it?

Sergeant   Come with us. We'll get it off you.

They take him off. **Mother Courage** *calls out after them.*

Mother Courage   He'd tell you! He's not that stupid! And don't break his arm.

She runs out after them.

Later. The evening of the same day. **The Chaplain** *and* **Kattrin** *are sharpening knives and washing glasses.*

The Chaplain   Cases like this where someone gets caught, well, they're not unknown in religious history. It's not unlike the Passion itself.

He sings.

At the first hour our good Lord stood
And prayed and watched by Pilate's side
And Pontius said he is not mine
Let Herod have him tried

He is not guilty Pontius said
But I refuse to say
Let him be tried by someone else
And then he turned away

At the third hour they took their whips
They scourged his side, the blood ran red
And then they took a crown of thorns
And placed it on his head

His heavy cross he had to bear
To carry on his own
His back bent low he made his way
To face his death alone

At the sixth hour they took his clothes
They nailed his body to the wood
And then they laughed because it was
A triumph over good

They jeered, they ran, they fled from him
No one remained to see
The sun go down, and darkness shroud
The man upon the tree

At the ninth hour he cried out loud
My God, why have you left my side?
He took a sponge with vinegar
He drank and then he died

The temple shook, the veil was rent
The earth was dark. One soldier stood
And from God's sides there flowed
Water mixed up with blood

At evening time they broke his legs
They stabbed him through with spears
Not once, not twice, but many times
To smother all their fears

They took his broken body then
Their happiness began
They had done what they had wanted to
A God who was a man.

As the song ends, **Mother Courage** *enters excitedly.*

Mother Courage   It's touch and go. The Sergeant'll listen
to reason. Only he mustn't know we're related to the boy, or
they'll say we helped him. It's a question of money, that's all.

I've had a word with Yvette. She's dug up some colonel. I'm going to see if he'll buy the business for her.

The Chaplain   Do you want to sell?

Mother Courage   Do I want to? What choice do I have?

The Chaplain   But how are you going to live?

Mother Courage   Well, that's it.

Yvette arrives with an extremely ancient **Colonel** *in tow. She embraces* **Mother Courage**.

Yvette   My dear Courage, how wonderful to see you again! (*Whispering.*) He didn't say no. (*Aloud again.*) This is my dear friend and business adviser. I was telling him that I'd heard by chance that you are selling your vehicle.

Mother Courage   Not selling, no. More leasing is what I had in mind.

Yvette (*disappointed*)   Oh only leasing. I thought you were going to sell.

Mother Courage   You're not going to find a cart like this every day.

Yvette   I'm not sure I'm interested if you're only leasing. (*To the* **Old Colonel**.) What do you think?

Old Colonel   Whatever you think, angel.

Yvette   I thought you needed money.

Mother Courage   I do need money. But I also need to live. Whichever, it's a real chance for you, Yvette. I mean, let's face it, who knows when you'll next meet another business adviser?

Yvette   I'm not sure. My friend wants me to have it, but not as a lease. He wants me to own it, don't you, sweetheart?

Old Colonel   I do. I do.

Mother Courage   Oh, well, then of course, if you want to *buy* something, you'll have to go on looking. I dare say in a week or two you might find the right thing.

Yvette   Then, surely, let's look. I love shopping.

Old Colonel   Do you, sweetheart?

Yvette   As much as I love being with you.

She turns back to **Mother Courage**.

If I give you the money, when will you pay it back?

Mother Courage   Two weeks perhaps. Maybe one.

Yvette   Oh I just can't decide. Advise me, *chéri*.

She takes the **Old Colonel** *to one side.*

She has to sell, don't worry. She has to.

Old Colonel   Well . . .

Yvette   And I do have to say, I mean I know I shouldn't tell you this, but I've had another offer. There's this lieutenant, kind of blond, big, you know? . . .

Old Colonel   Don't take his money, I beg you, my darling. He'll take advantage of you. I said I'd buy you something, didn't I?

Yvette   Well, I mean if you think the lieutenant might use me . . .

Old Colonel   He will. He will.

Yvette   Then all right, yes. If you say so. I don't want to take your money, sweet one. But I shall.

She turns back to **Mother Courage**.

I have discussed it with my friend and he has advised me to accept. Make out a chitty saying the wagon's mine if you fail to pay up in two weeks. With all the contents. I'm going to make a list. I'll bring the two hundred shillings later. (*To the*

Old Colonel.) You go back to the camp, I won't be long, I need to check there's nothing missing from my property.

He leaves. She climbs onto the cart.

Not many boots left, are there?

Mother Courage   Yvette, this is not the moment for a fucking inventory. You've got to negotiate for us with the Sergeant. The court martial's in just under an hour.

Yvette   I just want to count the shirts.

Mother Courage *pulls her down by her skirts.*

Mother Courage   Come down, you bloody hyena! My son's life is at stake! And not a word about where you got the money or else the Sergeant's going to suspect.

Yvette   I've arranged to meet that one-eyed bloke in the bushes. He's agreed to be the go-between.

The Chaplain   Don't give two hundred unless you have to. A hundred and fifty is where you should start.

Mother Courage   Shut your face, it's nothing to do with you. You'll be all right, whatever happens. Just run and don't haggle. Remember, it's life and death.

She pushes **Yvette** *off.*

The Chaplain   It's none of my business, but how are we going to survive? You can hardly put your daughter to work.

Mother Courage   I'm counting on the cash box, idiot. If we get to keep the cash box, we won't be down on the deal.

The Chaplain   Are you sure Yvette's up to all this?

Mother Courage   Why not? It's in her own interest. She thinks I won't be able to pay her back and that way she'll get her hands on the cart. Colonels don't last for ever. Kattrin, knives. There's the stone. And you, stop standing around like Jesus having twins. Get on with it, wash the glasses, there's at least fifty cavalry in tonight, and I don't want all that stuff about your poor feet and how you never had to run when you were in church. I think we'll get him back. Thank God they're corruptible. They're human and after money like the rest of us. They're not wolves. As long as there's corruption, there's hope. Bribes! They're a man's best chance. As long as judges go on taking money, then there's some chance of justice.

Yvette *enters, panting.*

Yvette They'll do it for two hundred. But it's got to be quick. It's soon going to be out of their hands. They tortured Swiss Cheese. He admitted he had the box. He said he chucked it in the river when he saw they were coming. What do I do? Take the Cyclops to get the money from my colonel?

Mother Courage He chucked it in the river? I don't believe it! How do I get my two hundred back?

Yvette Oh I see. Now I get it. That was the plan. Yeah, and I would have been left with nothing. Well, hard luck, forget it. You're going to have to pay if you want Swiss Cheese. Or perhaps you'd prefer I drop the whole thing?

Mother Courage It never occurred to me. Shit! You needn't worry, Yvette, you'll get your cart. I've only had it seventeen years. I need a moment to think. I can't pay two hundred. I can't. Without money, I'm nothing. Any stranger can kick me in the ditch. All right, say one twenty. Go back and say one twenty or the deal's off. Whatever happens, I lose the cart.

Yvette They're not going to take it. I warn you. The Cyclops is already getting jumpy. He needs the two hundred.

Mother Courage I can't. I can't give him that. I've worked thirty years. This girl is twenty-five and she has no husband. I've got to think of her. Don't argue, I know what I'm doing! One hundred and twenty or the deal's off.

Yvette You know best.

She rushes off. Without looking at **The Chaplain** *or at her daughter,* **Mother Courage** *sits down to help* **Kattrin** *polish knives.*

Mother Courage   Don't break the glasses, they're not ours any more. Watch what you're doing or you'll cut yourself. He will come back, I promise. I'll pay two hundred if I have to. You'll get your brother back. But if we keep eighty we can load a trunk with something. You have to start somewhere.

The Chaplain   It is written: the Lord will provide.

Mother Courage   Dry them properly.

They clean the knives in silence. Then **Yvette** *comes running on sobbing.*

Yvette   It's not going to work. I warned you. The Cyclops wanted to leave straight away. He says there's no point. Any minute now, you'll hear the drum and that means the sentence is passed. I offered him one fifty. Nothing. He didn't even want to stay while I came back.

Mother Courage   Tell him he gets the two hundred. Run!

Yvette *runs off.* **Mother Courage** *sits in silence.* **The Chaplain** *has stopped polishing.*

Mother Courage   Maybe I haggled too long.

The drums sound. **The Chaplain** *stands up and walks upstage.* **Mother Courage** *remains seated. It grows dark.*

The drums stop. It grows light again. **Mother Courage** *has not moved.* **Yvette** *appears, deathly pale.*

Yvette   Well, you got what you wanted. You keep your cart. Eleven bullets he got, that's all. I don't know why I've come back. I don't know why I still bother with you. But they're convinced the cash box isn't in the river. They think you've got it. They think you're his mother. They're bringing the body here. If you show you know him they'll kill you.

You might as well know they're right behind me. Shall I hide Kattrin?

Mother Courage *shakes her head.*

Yvette Perhaps she didn't hear the drums. Perhaps she didn't know what they meant.

Mother Courage She knows. Fetch her.

Yvette *fetches* **Kattrin** *who goes to her mother and stands by her side.* **Mother Courage** *takes her by the hand. Two* **Mercenaries** *come with a stretcher. Something on it is covered by a sheet. The* **Sergeant** *is with them. They put the stretcher down.*

Sergeant There's a man here we don't know. We need his name, for the record. He had a meal here. Take a look and see if you know him.

He pulls back the sheet.

Well?

Mother Courage *shakes her head.*

Sergeant You've never seen him before today.

Mother Courage *shakes her head again.*

Sergeant Pick him up. He's got no friends. Throw him on the fire.

They carry him off.

4 Poland. 1629.

Mother Courage *is waiting outside an officer's tent. The* **Regimental Clerk** *looks out of the tent.*

Regimental Clerk I know you. You run that canteen. The one where they found that young thief. I wouldn't advise you to start making complaints.

Mother Courage I've got to. They came and they slashed my cart with their sabres. They ruined my stock. And then they demanded a five-shilling fine. For nothing. If I didn't complain it would be like admitting I'd done something wrong.

Regimental Clerk   We're short of canteens, so we're prepared to let you go on trading. Specially if you pay a fine now and then. But if you take my advice, you'll say nothing.

Mother Courage   I'm here to complain.

Regimental Clerk   It's up to you. You must wait for the captain.

The **Regimental Clerk** *goes back into the tent as a* **Young Soldier** *comes in aggressively, pursued by an* **Older Soldier**.

Young Soldier   Bouque la Madonne! Where is that bastard of a captain? Spending my money on drink and on whores! I'll kill you.

Older Soldier   For God's sake, keep quiet. You'll end up in the stocks!

Young Soldier   Come on out, you thief! I'll slice you in pieces! Come out and fight me! You stole my reward!

Older Soldier   Pull yourself together, man. You're going to get yourself killed.

Mother Courage   Is this some reward he didn't get?

Young Soldier   As God is my witness, if you don't let go of me, I swear I'll kill you as well.

Older Soldier   He crossed a river to save the colonel's horse and then the colonel welched on the reward he'd promised. He's still young. He doesn't understand.

Mother Courage   Let him go. He's not like a dog, you have to keep him tied up.

Young Soldier   He's in there getting drunk! You're all trouser-shitters! I've done a great service and I want my reward!

Mother Courage   Young man, don't shout at me, I've got my own problems. Save your voice, you'll need it when the captain comes. You'll need some voice left for when he gets here. Else he won't be offended enough to put you in chains. I tell you, I've known a lot of shouters. It never lasts long. Half an hour's serious lung work and then you have to put them to bed.

Young Soldier   I'm not going to listen. This is an injustice and injustice is something I will not endure.

Mother Courage   Oh really? Gives you a problem, does it? Injustice? How long can't you put up with it for? Is an hour difficult? Or does it bug you for two? Because in the stocks, I tell you, there's this strange sort of moment when people suddenly think, oh perhaps I can put up with injustice after all.

Young Soldier   Why am I listening to this rubbish? Bouque la Madonne, where's that captain?

Mother Courage   You're listening to me because you know what I'm saying is true. Your anger has gone. It was only a short one. You need a long one. But long ones aren't always easy to find.

Young Soldier   Are you daring to tell me I don't deserve my reward?

Mother Courage   Not at all. Just the opposite. But I'm also saying your anger's too small. It won't get you anywhere. Not enough puff in it. If you had a big one, I'd be urging you on. Kill him, I'd say. I'd be telling you to do it. But if I encourage you and then you don't do it, then that's very dangerous, because, let's face it, the captain's going to start turning on me.

Older Soldier   You're right. It was only a tantrum.

Young Soldier   You say I'm not going to do it? Very well then, let's see.

He draws his sword dramatically. The **Regimental Clerk** *pokes his head out.*

Regimental Clerk   The captain will be out in one minute.
You over there, please sit down.

The **Young Soldier** *sits. The* **Regimental Clerk** *withdraws.*

Mother Courage   And down he goes. What did I tell you?
Armchair rebels! Sit down, they say, and we do. Nobody
ever started a revolution sitting down. No, don't stand up
again. Sad, but after what's happened it won't look the same.
And don't be embarrassed by what I think of you. Believe
me, I'm no different. They've bought us. They've bought our
spirit.

She sings.

When you're young and strong and fit
You find your anger
Your anger's what you cling to when you're young
I used to say: I won't, I shan't, piss off,
I'll do it, leave me, let me do it my way
I used to say: sod you, I'll do it how I want.

Not like the rest of my family. Please! High-minded, me, and
altogether superior. I'd read a book for a start!

Then the world comes
The world breathes
The world leans, you learn
The world knows
The world teaches
The world speaks in turn:

Just wait
You'll bend
In time
You'll find
The vows you make you'll break
To live
Just give
In doubt
Sell out
It's what God wants from you.

I mean, well, it's different when you've got children, isn't it?
Let's face it: no reason they should suffer for your principles.

> When you're old and fat and slow
> You lose your anger
> Your anger's what you ditch as time goes by
> You start to say: all right, that's it, I
> mean, why sure, don't even ask, I'll do it
> your way
> You start to say: it's fine, I'll do it
> how you want.

I mean, I'm not against people standing up for what they
believe in. Good luck to them. But let's be honest, it's only a
way of showing off, isn't it?

> Because the world comes
> The world breathes
> The world leans, you learn
> The world knows
> The world teaches
> The world speaks in turn:

> Just wait
> You'll bend
> In time
> You'll find
> The vows you make you'll break
> To live
> Just give
> In doubt
> Sell out
> It's what God wants from you.

Mother Courage (*to the* **Young Soldier**)   That's why I
think you should only take your sword out if you really mean
business and if your anger is big enough. Because if it isn't,
you might as well leave.

Young Soldier   Oh fuck off, bitch!

He stumbles away, the **Older Soldier** *following. The*
Regimental Clerk *sticks his head out.*

Regimental Clerk   The captain's ready. He'll hear your complaint.

Mother Courage   Thanks all the same. I've changed my mind.

She goes out.

5   Magdeburg, Saxony. 1631.

The aftermath of a battle. The cart is standing in the middle of a village which has been shot to pieces. In the distance thin victory music can be heard. Two **Soldiers** *are being served at the bar by* **Kattrin** *and* **Mother Courage**. *One of them has a woman's fur coat round his shoulders.*

Mother Courage   It's simple, I tell you. No money, no brandy.

Fur Coat   I want a drink.

Mother Courage   They're having the parade for their victory, but the one thing they don't do is pay their own men.

Fur Coat   It's not my fault, I was late for the looting. They only let us loot for an hour. The general was going round saying, I'm not some sort of inhuman monster. The town must have given him a bribe.

The Chaplain *staggers on.*

The Chaplain   There's still people left in the farmyard. The farmer's family. Somebody help me. I need some linen.

The **Second Soldier** *goes off with him.* **Kattrin** *becomes very agitated and tries to get her mother to give her cloth.*

Mother Courage   I haven't got any linen. I sold all my bandages. I'm not tearing up officers' shirts for that lot.

The Chaplain (*over his shoulder*)   I need linen, damn you.

Mother Courage *blocks* **Kattrin**'s *way onto the cart by sitting on the step.*

Mother Courage They're not having anything. They haven't got a penny. I know they can't pay.

The Chaplain *is bending over a woman he has carried on.*

The Chaplain Why did you stay on during the battle?

Farmer's Wife (*weakly*) Farm.

Mother Courage Well, that's it. That sums it all up. So bloody mean, they hang on to everything. And now it's me that's expected to pay.

Fur Coat It's their own fault for being Protestants.

Mother Courage It's not about being Protestant. It's about holding on to your farm.

Second Soldier Anyway, they're Catholics, as it happens.

Fur Coat Yeah, well, you always hit a few of your own.

The Chaplain *has brought in a* **Peasant**.

Peasant I've broken my arm.

The Chaplain Where's the linen?

Everyone looks at **Mother Courage** *who still does not move.*

Mother Courage Nothing doing. I can't afford it. I've taxes, I've duties, I've bribes, I've interest to pay.

Kattrin, *making terrible noises, lifts a plank and threatens her mother with it.*

Mother Courage Are you crazy? Put that plank down or I'll smash your face in, you cow. I'm not giving a penny. I don't want to. I've got to look after myself.

The Chaplain *lifts her up and puts her on the ground. Then he gets shirts and starts tearing them into strips.*

Mother Courage Those are my fucking shirts! They're half a shilling a piece.

A child is heard crying inside the house.

Peasant The baby's still in there.

Kattrin *rushes in as* **The Chaplain** *holds back the woman.*

The Chaplain Stay where you are, they'll get him out.

Mother Courage Stop her! That roof's falling in!

The Chaplain I'm not going back in there.

Mother Courage *is now torn between the house and the shirts which* **The Chaplain** *is tearing vigorously apart.*

Mother Courage And stop using so much!

The **Second Soldier** *holds her back.* **Kattrin** *brings a baby out of the ruins.*

Mother Courage Oh great, now you've found another baby to drag around with you. Give it to its mother at once, or are we going to fight for an hour to get it off you, like we did last time?

She turns angrily to the **Second Soldier**.

Don't stand there. Tell them to stop that bloody music. We don't need to be told it's a victory. We know it's a victory, we can see. I've got nothing but losses from your bloody victory.

The Chaplain The blood's coming through.

He is bandaging, as **Kattrin** *rocks the baby, singing a lullaby.*

Mother Courage Look at her! Happy as a lark, in all this misery. You give it back.

She discovers **Fur Coat** *has been rifling the drinks, and is now trying to make off with the bottle.*

Mother Courage You cheap crook, you thief. You pay for that.

Fur Coat I've nothing. I can't pay.

Mother Courage *tears the fur coat off his back.*

Mother Courage   Then leave us the coat. It's stolen anyway.

As she rolls up the coat and throws it into the cart, **Kattrin** *lifts the baby in the air. Both women have their share of the spoils.*

The Chaplain   There's still someone in there.

6   Ingolstadt, Bavaria. 1632.

The funeral of the Imperial Commander Tilly is going on outside a canteen tent. Inside, there is a bar at the back. It is raining. Drums and funeral music can be heard. For **Mother Courage**, *a time of prosperity.* **The Chaplain** *is playing a board game with the* **Regimental Clerk**. **Mother Courage** *and* **Kattrin** *are stocktaking.*

The Chaplain   The funeral procession should be moving off now.

Mother Courage   Shame about the Commander-in-Chief – twenty-two pairs of socks – they say the fog was to blame. He'd been shouting at some other regiment that it was their duty to fight to the death. He set off to go back to headquarters, lost his way in the mist, and accidentally went forwards instead of back. Ended up with a bullet in his throat. Only four lanterns left.

A **Soldier** *whistles for service. She goes to the counter.*

Mother Courage   It's a scandal, you lot skipping your own Commander's funeral.

She pours the men drinks.

Regimental Clerk   The mistake was giving the men the money before the ceremony. Now they're all getting drunk rather than go.

The Chaplain   Shouldn't you be there?

Regimental Clerk   I wanted to. But the rain. You know.

Mother Courage   Yeah, well, fair enough, your uniform
might get wet. I hear they wanted the church bells rung but
as the Commander had ordered all the churches to be
destroyed the poor chap's going to miss out. They are going
to fire a few rounds, though, that should cheer things up.
Seventeen belts.

Shouts (*from the bar*)   Come on! Service! Brandy!

Mother Courage   Let's see your money. Hey, you, you're
not coming in here in those boots. You can drink outside,
rain or no rain.

She goes back to the **Regimental Clerk**.

It's officers only, as far as I'm concerned.

The Chaplain   They must be filing past the body now.

Mother Courage   You have to feel sorry for them, don't
you? I mean all these commanders and emperors, trying to
do something marvellous which will make them remembered
for hundreds of years. All they want is to become a statue, or
conquer the world or something, some reasonable ambition
like that, and it all goes wrong because of these stupid bog-
ordinary people who only want a glass of beer and a chit-
chat. No sense of the higher things in life! Even emperors
can't do it all by themselves. They have to depend on these
hopelessly inadequate things called people to carry out all
their wonderful plans. And they don't. Am I right?

The Chaplain *laughs*.

The Chaplain   Courage, you're right. Except about the
soldiers. If you take those men out there, drinking their
brandy in the rain, I promise you they'll fight. And they'll go
on fighting. These are men who won't stop, if need be, for
two hundred years.

Mother Courage   Seventeen buckles. Then it's not your
opinion the war might end?

The Chaplain   What, just because the Commander-in-
Chief has died? Don't be absurd. There are dozens of them.
There's always more heroes.

Mother Courage   I'm not asking for the sake of it. I'm asking because there's a whole lot of stuff on the market. Not much point in investing if the war's going to end.

The Chaplain   I know why you're asking. There are always people going round saying 'Oh the war will end one day.' I say, no. Actually, there's no reason it should ever end. Of course there'll be lulls, the war will take a breather now and again – after all, nothing on this earth is perfect – not even war. I doubt if there'll be a perfect war, not one of which you could truly say 'This one's really got nothing wrong with it.' All of a sudden this war may stop. For no apparent reason. Just come to a halt. Like that. Of its own volition. But when it does, you may be sure there'll be plenty of people to get it going again. A king or a pope or an emperor. Oh yes, a war always has friends.

A **Soldier** *sings at the bar.*

Soldier
    A brandy, landlord, please make haste
    A soldier has no time to waste.

Make it a double as it's a holiday!

Mother Courage   If only I could be sure you're right.

The Chaplain   Think it out for yourself. How can the war end?

The **Soldier** *sings to* **Kattrin** *who smiles back at him.*

Soldier
    Your breast, my love, oh please make haste
    A soldier has no time to waste.

Regimental Clerk (*suddenly*)   But what about peace? I'm from Bohemia. I'd like to go home occasionally.

The Chaplain   Oh would you indeed? Ah yes, peace. But where is the hole once the cheese has been eaten?

Soldier
    Play trumps, my friend, please make haste
    A soldier has no time to waste
    He hears his Emperor's cry

Your prayers, priest, and please make haste
A soldier has no time to waste
The Emperor bids him die.

Regimental Clerk   I mean, in the long run, you can't live
without peace.

The Chaplain   Of course. But there's peace in war,
remember. It has its little islands of peace. War satisfies all
needs, that's the whole secret of its appeal. Even in a war,
you can always stop for a crap. Between battles you can
always have a beer. On a march, you can always have a
snooze. It's possible. Of course you can't get a full game of
cards during an invasion, but frankly nor can you at harvest
time. Sure, you may lose a leg, and at first, well of course,
you'll do a certain amount of yelling and shouting, but then
they bring you brandy, you take hopping lessons, and the
war's none the worse for your mishap. And best of all, in the
middle of the slaughter, you can always stop and do some
random reproducing. Behind a barn, say. And then the war
will have your children, and feed off them as well. War's like
love. It finds a way. Why should it ever end?

Kattrin *has stopped working, deeply affected by what he has said.
She stares at* **The Chaplain**.

Mother Courage   OK, fair enough. I'm going to buy that
stuff after all.

Kattrin *suddenly bangs down a basket of glasses on the ground and
runs out.* **Mother Courage** *laughs.*

Mother Courage   Kattrin! Oh Lord Jesus, you've upset
her. All she wants is the peace, because I promised her then
she can have a husband.

She runs after **Kattrin**.

Regimental Clerk   I've won. You were too busy talking.
Pay up.

Mother Courage *comes back with* **Kattrin**.

Mother Courage Come on, don't worry. The war'll go on a bit longer, we'll make a bit more money, and peace'll be all the nicer when it comes. Now you go off to the town, get that stuff we reserved at the tavern. Just bring the valuables, the rest we can pick up later in the cart. It's all fixed, the regimental clerk here's going with you. Everyone's at the funeral, so you're perfectly safe. Don't let anyone steal from you, you need it for your dowry, isn't that right?

Kattrin *puts a cloth over her head and leaves with the* **Regimental Clerk**.

The Chaplain You trust the clerk with her?

Mother Courage Oh sure. She's not pretty enough that anyone's going to bother with her.

The Chaplain It's admirable the way you run your business. The way you always come through. I see how you got your name.

Mother Courage My name? Ah. Well, you don't have much choice, do you? Not when you're poor. The world's run by popes and emperors. And they need people to fight their wars for them. Courage? Oh sure.

She sits down and takes out a little pipe from her pocket and smokes.

You could chop a bit of firewood.

The Chaplain *unwillingly takes off his jacket and prepares to chop wood.*

The Chaplain Properly, I'm a pastor of souls, not a lumberjack.

Mother Courage I don't have a soul. But I do need firewood.

The Chaplain Have I seen that stumpy little pipe of yours before?

Mother Courage It's just a pipe.

The Chaplain It seems to me a very particular pipe.

Mother Courage Perhaps.

The Chaplain   It's the cook's pipe. The cook from the Oxenstierna Regiment.

Mother Courage   If you knew already, why did you ask?

The Chaplain   Because I wasn't sure if you knew. I mean, if it was an accident. If you were rummaging around and came up with that knobbly old pipe by chance.

Mother Courage   What if I did?

The Chaplain *brings the axe down with a huge blow.*

Mother Courage   What if I know what I'm doing?

The Chaplain   Courage, I'm warning you. It's my duty. I'm sure you'll never see that gentleman again, and if so, you can be grateful because he gave me the impression of not being entirely reliable. Quite the opposite.

Mother Courage   He was charming, though.

The Chaplain   Charming? No, I would not call him charming. I wish him no ill, but I would call him a Don Juan. Look at the pipe, if you don't believe me. The pipe will tell you all you need to know.

Mother Courage   All I can see is it's been used.

The Chaplain   More than used. It's been bitten right through. That is the pipe of an angry, ruthless brute and if you had any judgement left towards him you would see that quite clearly.

He delivers another huge blow with the axe.

Mother Courage   You're going to split my chopping-block in half!

The Chaplain   I told you, I did not train as a woodcutter but as a pastor of souls. Here in this place, doing this demeaning work, my talents are squandered. The gifts God gave me are not allowed to shine. Waste is a sin. You have yet to hear me preach. In a single sermon I can so fire up a regiment that they will go among the enemy and destroy them like a flock of sheep. They will throw away their own lives, as if casting aside a stinking footcloth, at the thought of final victory. God has granted me the power of divine eloquence. I can preach till you lose all sight and hearing.

Mother Courage I'm not sure I want to lose sight and hearing. I mean, what'd be the point?

The Chaplain Courage, I have often thought that your harsh exterior conceals a warm heart. And more. You too are human and need warmth.

Mother Courage Well certainly if we want this tent warm the best way's to chop wood.

The Chaplain (*smiling at this tactic*) Please. I sometimes ask myself how it would be for us if we were to draw closer. Given that the whirlwind of war has already thrown us strangely together.

Mother Courage I'd say we were close enough. I cook your meals and in return you sometimes get quite close to chopping wood.

He moves towards her, the axe still in his hand.

The Chaplain I think you know what I mean by 'closer'. It has nothing to do with vulgar things like wood and food. Listen to your own heart!

Mother Courage If you could just mind what you do with that axe. I think you may be getting a little too close.

The Chaplain You make everything a joke. I am serious and sincere. I know what I want.

Mother Courage Chaplain, come on, be sensible. I like you. The last thing I want is to have to be angry with you. All I want is to get me and my children through this war. And this cart as well, which isn't just mine. I've no wish for a life of my own. Right now I'm taking a terrible risk by buying in when the Commander has just died and all the talk is of peace. That's a risk. Where will you go if I'm ruined? You don't know, do you?

There's a silence. He can't answer.

Chop us some wood, then we'll be warm in the evenings, and
that's not nothing these days. What was that?

She suddenly gets up. **Kattrin** *comes on breathless, a terrible wound
over her eye and forehead. She is carrying a whole mixture of things:
parcels, leather goods, a drum.*

Mother Courage   What's happened? Did they get you? On
the way home? They got her on the way home. It was that
soldier, I know it was, the one who was drinking in here. I
should never have let you go. For Christ's sake, put that stuff
down. It really isn't bad, it's only a flesh wound. I'll bandage
it for you. In a week it'll be gone.

She starts to bandage the wound.

They're worse than animals.

The Chaplain   It's not their fault. I don't blame them.
Back at home they don't rape. It's the war. It's the people
who run the war. It's anyone who starts a war.

Mother Courage   That bloody clerk! Why didn't he walk
back with you? I suppose he thought you'd be safe. You look
respectable. It's going to be all right, it's not going to show.

She has finished bandaging.

Now stay there, keep calm, I've got something for you. A
secret. It's something I've kept for you.

She digs **Yvette***'s red boots out of a bag.*

Here. Yes. There we are. You always wanted them. Well,
now they're yours. Get them on quick, before I change my
mind. It's going to be all right, really. It's not going to show.
Mind you, it won't be a disaster if it does. Means at least
they'll leave you alone. It's the pretty ones they go for, it's
the pretty ones who have to spend this war on their backs.
No time at all, their looks are gone, and they're frightened to
walk down the street. It's like with trees. You know. It's the
tall straight ones, they're the ones that get chopped down
and turned into planks. The crooked ones nobody bothers
with. They're left in peace to get on and grow. So look at it

that way, you could call it luck. The boots are good, I greased them before I put them away.

Kattrin *leaves the boots where they are and creeps into the cart.*

The Chaplain   Let's hope she won't be disfigured.

Mother Courage   That scar is for life. No point in her waiting for peace any more.

The Chaplain   She didn't let them steal the stuff.

Mother Courage   Maybe I shouldn't have gone on about that. If only I knew what goes on in her head! Just once she stayed out all night. Just once, in all these years. She never told me what happened. Afterwards, she began to work harder, that's all. It worried me. I couldn't put it out of my mind.

She collects the goods **Kattrin** *has brought and angrily begins to sort them out.*

That's war for you. A nice way to make a living!

There is the sound of cannon fire.

The Chaplain   The Commander's being buried. This is a moment in history.

Mother Courage   History? What I call history's when my daughter gets hit in the eye. She's already half-knackered. She'll never get a husband, and her so mad about kids. She's only dumb because of the war. A soldier stuffed something in her mouth when she was young. As for Swiss Cheese, I'll never see him again. Where Eilif is, God alone knows. Damn the fucking war!

7   On the Road. 1632.

At once, music. Now, in immediate contrast to the previous scene, **Mother Courage** *is at the height of her business career.* **The Chaplain,** **Mother Courage** *and* **Kattrin** *are pulling the cart. It*

is laden with new goods. **Mother Courage** *herself is wearing a
necklace of silver coins and bracelets.*

Mother Courage   I'm not having anyone put me off this
war. They keep saying, war destroys the weak. I don't notice
the weak doing so brilliantly during the peace. It's war that
feeds its own!

She sings.

> Nobody try and tell me this is different
> War's a business and it's just like all the rest
> All right, we have to deal in guns and bullets
> But it's still about survival of the best.

And what good is ducking out anyway? The ones who duck
out are the first ones to get killed.

> Nobody needs to go and be a martyr
> If you're clever then there's no need to be brave
> Keep moving, keep buying, keep selling, keep killing
> The only peace you'll find is in the grave.

They pull the cart on its way.

> The war goes on. The war is raging.
> The men are here. They must be fed
> And what remains must now start trading
> That's us. Let's go. It's going well.

8   Saxony. 1632.

*A summer morning. The cart is parked in a military camp. In front of
it, a* **Young Man** *and an* **Old Woman** *are standing. The* **Young
Man** *has a large bag of bedding.* **Mother Courage***'s voice comes
from inside the wagon.*

Mother Courage (*off*)   Do we really have to do this at the
crack of dawn?

Young Man   We walked through the night to get here. And
we have to go back today.

Mother Courage (*off*)   Who wants to buy bedding? When people don't have houses to live in.

Young Man   You might at least take a look.

Old Woman   It's hopeless. We should go home.

Young Man   What are you saying, Ma? If we don't make this sale we lose our house for taxes. She still might give us three shillings if you throw in your bracelet.

Bells begin to ring.

What on earth's going on?

Voices (*from the back*)   It's peace! Peace! The King of Sweden's been killed.

Mother Courage *sticks her head out from the cart. She hasn't yet done her hair.* **The Chaplain** *crawls out from under the cart.*

Mother Courage   What are they ringing bells for? It isn't Sunday.

The Chaplain   What are they saying?

Young Man   It's peace.

Mother Courage   Oh no, not an outbreak of peace. Just when I've bought in new stock.

The Chaplain *is calling up at the back.*

The Chaplain   Is it true? Is it peace?

Voice (*from a distance*)   It's true. It happened three weeks ago. It's just nobody told us.

The Chaplain (*to* **Mother Courage**)   It's wonderful. Of course! Why else would they be ringing the bells?

Voices   There's a whole lot of Lutherans, just arrived in town. They brought the news.

Young Man   Ma, it's peace, it's peace at last. What's wrong?

The **Old Woman** *has collapsed.* **Mother Courage** *is speaking into the cart.*

Mother Courage (*off*)   Kattrin, it's peace. It's happened. Put on your black dress. We're going to church, we owe it to Swiss Cheese. Is it true, though?

Young Man   Everyone's saying it. Can you stand up?

The **Old Woman** *gets up stunned.*

Young Man   I can start making saddles again, I promise you. And father will get his bed back. Do you think you can walk?

He turns to **The Chaplain**.

The news was too much for her. She never thought it could happen. But my father believed it. My father is a man who never lost faith.

They head back home.

Mother Courage (*off*)   Give the woman a brandy!

The Chaplain   They've already gone.

Mother Courage (*off*)   What's going on in the camp?

The Chaplain   There's some sort of meeting. I think I'll go over. Do you think I should put on my pastor's coat?

Mother Courage (*off*)   I wouldn't go that far. I'd make further inquiries before you dress up as the Antichrist. I'm pleased if it's true, even though I'm ruined. At least I got two of my kids through the war. And at last I'll see Eilif.

The Chaplain   Oh no, look who's coming.

The Cook *appears, somewhat bedraggled and carrying a bundle.*

The Cook   Well, stone me! It's the bloody Chaplain!

The Chaplain   Mother Courage, I'm afraid we've got guests.

Mother Courage *climbs out of the cart.*

Mother Courage   Cooky, my God! I don't believe it. How long has it been?

66

The Cook I never break a promise. Four years ago I said I'd come back. For a chat and a glass of brandy.

Mother Courage Have you seen Eilif?

The Cook Of course. I thought he'd be here. He left before me. On his way to find you.

The Chaplain I don't care, I'm going to wear my proper clothes.

He disappears behind the cart to change.

Mother Courage Then he'll be here any minute.

She calls into the cart.

Kattrin, your brother's on the way. Get Cook a glass of brandy, Kattrin.

Kattrin *does not appear.*

Mother Courage Put your hair over it, no one'll see it. Cook's an old friend.

But she has to get the brandy herself.

She won't come out. Peace means nothing to her. She waited too long. She took a blow. Over the eye. The truth is, you can hardly see it, but she's convinced that everyone's looking at her all the time.

The Cook Ah yes. War.

The two of them sit together on a bench.

Mother Courage Well, Cooky, no question you find me at a bad moment. It looks like I'm ruined.

The Cook How come?

Mother Courage I took the Chaplain's advice. He told me the war wouldn't end, so I built up my stocks. Now I'm left holding the stuff.

The Cook How could you? I was going to warn you that day. Only the Catholics arrived so quickly, I got no chance. The man's an obvious parasite.

Mother Courage   He's been washing the dishes. He helps pull the cart.

The Cook   Him pull? Who are you kidding? And what's more I'm sure he's been telling you some of his so-called jokes. He's got a very unhealthy view of women. I tried to exert some influence, but it was no use. He isn't steady.

Mother Courage   And are you steady?

The Cook   Whatever else, steady. Cheers!

Mother Courage   I'm not sure steady's so wonderful. I've only been with one steady man, thank God. I've never been so bored in my life. He called my way of life distinctly unchristian. I don't think I'll try steady again.

The Cook   Ah, you don't change. That wonderful toughness. I love that in you.

Mother Courage   Don't say you've been dreaming of my toughness.

The Cook   So here we are then, in our hands a glass of your famous brandy. And the bells of peace ringing at last.

Mother Courage   I can't say I give a toss for the bells. Not unless the soldier's are going to get back pay. Have you been paid off?

The Cook (*hesitating*)   Well no, not exactly. In point of fact, to be honest, that's why we left. I thought, right, I'll go and see my friend Anna Fierling.

Mother Courage   In other words, you're broke.

The Cook *is now irritated by the bells.*

The Cook   That's enough bells, you're right, they've made their point. The fact is, I'd quite like to set up in business myself. I've had enough of being a cook. Trying to make soup from tree roots and old leather. You serve it, they throw it back in your face. You're actually better off as a soldier. But of course now it's too late.

The Chaplain *reappears in his old clerical clothes.*

The Cook Let's talk it over later.

The Chaplain This coat's pretty good. Just a few moth holes.

The Cook I don't know why you think you're going to get your job back. Sending innocent people to their death.

The Chaplain That's not what I did.

The Cook Handing out more of your rotten advice. Like telling this poor woman to invest all her money because the war was bound to go on.

The Chaplain (*furious*) I hardly see it's any of your business.

The Cook I think it may well be my business.

The Chaplain (*to* **Mother Courage**) I didn't know this man was such a close friend of yours that you had to answer to him.

Mother Courage No need to get so rattled, the Cook's only saying what he thinks. And you must admit this war has turned into a bit of a flop.

The Chaplain How dare you? How dare you blaspheme against peace? Courage, you are a hyena of the battlefield.

Mother Courage I'm a what?

The Cook Insult this woman, and you'll answer to me.

The Chaplain No. It's not you I'm speaking to. It's quite clear what you're doing here. (*He turns to* **Mother Courage**.) But when I see you take hold of this peace like a snotty old handkerchief . . . I'm sorry, something in me – call it my humanity – yes, my humanity rebels. You thrive on war. You actually prefer it. Because money's the only thing you love. But may I remind you of a saying 'He who sups with the devil needs a long spoon'?

Mother Courage   I've no love of war, and war's shown little enough love for me. I'm not even going to argue. You call me a hyena, and as far as I'm concerned that's it.

The Chaplain   Why are you complaining about peace? How dare you? For a few pieces of rubbish in the back of your cart?

Mother Courage   My goods have never been rubbish. They're what I live on. And what you were living on until about five minutes ago.

The Chaplain   Exactly! You live off the war.

The Cook (*to* **The Chaplain**)   You're old enough to know by now: it's always a mistake to offer anyone advice. (*To* **Mother Courage**.) Your best chance, I'd say, is start offloading stuff at once. The sooner the better, there's not a moment to lose.

Mother Courage   That's it, absolutely. I'm going to get going at once.

The Chaplain   Oh yes! Because Cooky says so!

Mother Courage   It doesn't matter who says so, just as long as they're right.

She gets into the cart to prepare for market.

The Cook   Round One to me, Padre. I must say, you're not very good in an argument. You didn't say the right thing at all. You should have said, 'I wasn't advising you on matters of business. I was just talking politics.' That's what you should have said.

The Chaplain   If you don't shut your mouth, I swear to God I'll kill you, cassock or not.

The Cook *pulls off his boots and unwraps his footcloths.*

The Cook   It's a shame. If you hadn't become such a hopeless fucker, you'd get a nice parish now peace is here. People don't need cooks, there's nothing to cook, but they go on believing, nothing's changed there.

The Chaplain Cook, I have to ask you not to force me out of here. Since I went on the road, I believe I've become a better person. If you want the truth, I don't think I could preach to anyone now.

Yvette Pottier *comes in, dressed to the nines, in black. She is so fat eating seems to have become her only passion. She is followed by a* **Servant**.

Yvette Pardon me, is this Mother Courage's establishment?

The Chaplain Indeed yes it is. And with whom do we have the honour?

Yvette I am the wife of Colonel Starhemberg. Is Mother Courage receiving visitors?

The Chaplain *calls into the cart.*

The Chaplain The wife of Colonel Starhemberg to see you!

Mother Courage (*off*) I'm coming.

Yvette It's Yvette.

Mother Courage (*off*) Yvette!

Yvette Just called round to see how you are.

The Cook *turns round in horror.*

Yvette Pieter!

The Cook Yvette!

Yvette What are you doing here?

The Chaplain Are you two friends? I mean, are you close friends?

Yvette Just about as close as it gets.

She looks **The Cook** *over.*

You've got fat.

The Cook Well, you're not exactly undernourished yourself.

Yvette It's great to see you, arsehole. I've waited half my life to tell you what I think of you.

The Chaplain Excellent. But, better still, wait till Mother Courage is here.

Mother Courage *appears loaded down with stuff from the cart. They embrace.*

Mother Courage Yvette! But why are you in mourning?

Yvette Don't you think it suits me? My husband, the colonel, died several years ago.

Mother Courage The one who nearly bought my cart?

Yvette Well, no. His elder brother.

Mother Courage So you've done pretty well. Thank God. At least someone's done well from the war.

Yvette Not entirely. It's been up and down, as they say.

Mother Courage I won't hear a word against colonels. In my experience they're never short of a bob.

The Chaplain *turns to* **The Cook**.

The Chaplain If I were you, I'd put my shoes back on again. (*To* **Yvette**.) You promised you'd give us your opinion of this gentleman.

The Cook Yvette, there's no need to start stirring things up.

Mother Courage This man is a friend of mine, Yvette.

Yvette Haven't you got it? This man, as you call him, is Piet the Pipe.

Mother Courage (*laughing*) You mean the one who used to drive women crazy?

The Cook I'm not Piet the bloody Pipe. I happen to have a proper name, thank you.

Mother Courage And it's me that's been looking after the bloody pipe!

The Chaplain And smoking it.

Yvette Yeah, well, it's lucky I'm here to warn you against him. He's had half the women in Flanders.

The Cook That was a long time ago. And it's not true.

Yvette You should stand when a lady's addressing you. Oh God, I really did love this man! And he was off all the time debauching some bandy-legged brunette. He banged her up as well.

The Cook It seems to me you haven't done badly out of it.

Yvette How dare you, you prick? Anna, be careful, his type's still dangerous, even when they've lost their looks.

Mother Courage Come on, we need to get this stuff shifted. I'm hoping you're going to know a few people who might be in a position to buy.

She calls into the cart.

Kattrin, forget the church, I'm off to market. When Eilif gets here, give him a nice drink.

She starts to leave with **Yvette** *who is still complaining.*

Yvette Look at him. The source of all my misfortunes! All right, I've had some luck since. But if I can just stop one poor innocent virgin falling into his grubby clutches, then the Lord God will surely reward me in heaven.

They go.

The Chaplain I take as my text 'The mills of God grind exceedingly slowly.' And to think you dared to complain about my jokes!

The Cook I know, all right. I can see it, I'm buggered. I came here, I thought I might at least get a hot dinner. But now . . . after all that, she's got the wrong impression. I think I might as well move on.

The Chaplain Good idea.

The Cook   I tell you, this peace is a non-starter. It's not how we're meant to live. Man is born in sin. Our natural elements are fire and the sword. I'd give anything to be back with my general, chasing a big fat chicken, yellow with fat, putting it on the fire with mustard and carrot . . .

The Chaplain   Red cabbage. Red cabbage with chicken.

The Cook   I know. But he insisted on carrots.

The Chaplain   What did he know?

The Cook   It never stopped you tucking in.

The Chaplain   I ate under protest.

The Cook   You must admit those were the days.

The Chaplain   They were. I admit it.

The Cook   And now you've called her a hyena, I don't think you've any better chance round here than I have.

But **The Chaplain** *is not listening.*

The Cook   What are you staring at?

The Chaplain   It's Eilif!

Eilif *is being led in by* **Soldiers** *with pikes. His hands are tied. He is deathly pale, but he is in expensive clothing. The war has made him rich.*

The Chaplain   What on earth's going on?

Eilif   Is Ma around?

The Chaplain   She's gone into town.

Eilif   I'm allowed one last visit. That's what I'm doing here.

The Cook   Where are you taking him?

Soldier   Nowhere you'd want to go.

The Chaplain Why? I mean, what's he meant to have done?

Soldier Looted. Pillaged a farm. And then he murdered the farmer's wife.

The Chaplain Eilif, how could you do that?

Eilif I've done it before.

The Cook But that was war. That was during the war.

Eilif Oh yeah? And there's a difference? I want to sit down till she gets here.

Soldier We haven't got time.

The Chaplain During the war that was what he was honoured for. He was at his Commander's right hand. Then the name for it was heroism. The very same deed. Is there no appeal?

Soldier It's too late. Stealing a peasant's cattle, murdering his wife, why's that meant to be heroic?

The Cook It isn't heroic. It's stupid.

Eilif Yeah, well if I hadn't been stupid, I would have starved, dickhead.

The Cook Yeah, and because you're so clever, you're now going to die.

The Chaplain We must get Kattrin out to say goodbye to him.

Eilif No, leave her! Just give me a brandy.

Soldier Come on, there's no time for brandy.

The Chaplain Wait, hold on. What will we say to your mother?

Eilif   I don't know. Tell her . . . tell her anything. Tell her what you like. Tell her nothing. Oh for Christ's sake, tell her nothing at all.

The **Soldiers** *push him off.*

The Chaplain   Please. Let me come with you.

Eilif   I don't need a priest.

The Chaplain   No one can say that for sure.

He heads off with them but **The Cook** *shouts after him.*

The Cook   I'm going to have to tell her. She's bound to want to see him.

The Chaplain   No, leave it. Don't say anything for now. Just say he was here and she'll see him tomorrow. By then I'll be back. It's better I tell her. Please, Cooky, it's my job. Let me be the one.

He hurries off. **The Cook** *watches them go, shakes his head, then walks about uneasily. At last he approaches the cart.*

The Cook   Kattrin! What is it? Are you frightened of the peace? I don't blame you, I am as well. I'm the general's cook, you remember me? I was wondering if you had something I could eat. Maybe bacon. Bread. Bread would do just as well. I might as well eat. Just to pass the time.

He looks inside.

She's got a blanket over her head.

At once the sound of cannon fire resumes. **Mother Courage** *comes running on, out of breath and still with all her goods.*

Mother Courage   Cooky, it's over. The peace is over. The war's been on again for three days, they say. Lucky I heard before selling my stuff. You know the Lutherans who brought them the news? Well, now they've started killing them. We need to get this cart on the road. Kattrin, get packing! What are you looking like that for? What's going on?

The Cook   Nothing.

76

Mother Courage   I know there's something. I can see it in your eyes.

The Cook   Probably it's just the war starting. It could be tomorrow before I get a hot meal.

Mother Courage   Cooky, I know you're not telling me the truth.

The Cook   Eilif was here. But he had to move on straightaway.

Mother Courage   He was here? Well, that's great. I'll see him on the march. I've decided I'm going to change sides again. Back with our own lot. How does he look?

The Cook   Same as ever.

Mother Courage   He never changes. And the war won't get Eilif, he's far too smart. Are you going to help me pack?

She starts work herself.

What was his news? Is he still as popular as ever? Has he been doing great things?

The Cook (*darkly*)   He's certainly done one.

Mother Courage   I can't wait to hear.

Kattrin *appears.*

Mother Courage   Kattrin, peace is over, it's time to move on.

The Cook *hasn't moved.*

Mother Courage   What has got into you?

The Cook   I suppose I'm going to have to go and enlist.

Mother Courage   Where's the Chaplain?

The Cook   He's with Eilif. They went into town.

Mother Courage   Then why don't you join us? I mean, just for a while. I could do with some help.

The Cook   That stuff with Yvette . . .

Mother Courage   That did you no harm in my estimation. Far from it. Where there's smoke there's fire, at least that's what I'm hoping. Coming?

The Cook   I wouldn't say no.

Mother Courage   The Twelfth have moved off already. You'd better get into the yoke. Here's a hunk of bread to keep you going. Just think: I might see Eilif tonight. You know, he's my favourite of all of them. Well, the peace was short, wasn't it? And so on we go.

She readies the cart for departure, not knowing she will ride over **Eilif**'s *grave. She sings as* **The Cook** *and* **Kattrin** *harness themselves in.*

> Nobody thinks the war has yet been glutted
> It's time to feed the war with yet more men
> It eats and pretty soon it shits them
> Then finds a thousand more and starts again
> It's a hundred miles before we're out of Saxony
> The war's now lasted thirteen years or so
> So work it out! It hardly needs explaining
> With luck we've still got twenty years to go.

9   Fichtel Mountains, Saxony. 1634.

Two years later. It is autumn. There is famine and plague. The war is sixteen years old and half of Germany is wiped out. **Mother Courage** *and* **The Cook** *are in shabby sheepskins with the cart, in front of a half-ruined parsonage. There are no goods left on the cart.*

The Cook   There are no lights on. No one's up yet.

Mother Courage   If it's the parsonage, he's going to have to get up. He's going to have to leave his duvet to ring the bells. Then he'll have some hot soup.

The Cook   The whole village is burnt.

Mother Courage   There's people still there. I heard a dog bark.

The Cook   If the parson's got soup, he's not going to give it away.

Mother Courage   Perhaps if we sang . . .

The Cook   I'm tired of it. I can't take any more.

He unharnesses himself morosely. He takes out a letter.

I didn't tell you. I've had this letter. My mother's died of the cholera. I've inherited the inn. If you don't believe me, you can read it though it's none of your business, my aunt going on about the way I live and so on.

She reads the letter.

Mother Courage   I'm the same. I've had enough of the road. I'm like the butcher's dog, I deliver the meat, but I never get any myself. I've nothing to sell, and nobody has any money to buy. The other day someone tried to give me a pile of books for two eggs. In Wurtemburg I had a bag of salt, and all I was offered was a plough. What good's a plough? Nothing grows any more, except thorns. In Pomerania they say they're eating their own children. Someone saw a nun looting.

The Cook   The world's dying out.

Mother Courage   Sometimes I see myself driving my cart through hell selling brimstone, or through heaven ladling out lunch to wandering souls. If I could just take my two children to a place where there's no shooting, then we could just live for a while.

The Cook   Anna, I'm saying we can run this inn together. Last night I made up my mind. I'm going back to Utrecht, with you or without you. Today.

Mother Courage   I must talk to Kattrin. It's sudden. I don't like making decisions in the cold or when I'm hungry.

Kattrin *climbs down from the cart.*

Mother Courage   Kattrin, now listen. The Cook and I are thinking of going to Utrecht. He's been left an inn. You'd be staying in one place and meeting new people. There's a lot of men would be happy with a slightly older woman. Looks aren't everything, either. It would be good news for me, I get on well with Cooky, he's good at business. And we'd actually be fed. Even better, you'd have your own bed. Let's face it, when it comes down to it, this is no life, on the road. It's dangerous. You're already covered with lice. And we have to decide pretty quickly. The Swedes are heading north. They're somewhere over there.

She points left.

My view is, we should do it. We should go to Utrecht.

The Cook   Anna, I need a word with you alone.

Mother Courage   Kattrin, go back inside.

Kattrin *climbs back in.*

The Cook   I'm afraid you haven't quite understood me. I didn't think I'd have to spell it out like this. There's no question of her coming with us. Do you understand what I mean?

Kattrin *has stuck her head out the back of the cart and is listening.*

Mother Courage   I'd have to leave Kattrin behind?

The Cook   What do you think? It's a tiny place. If two of us work hard, we can make a living. But it can't support three. You can give her the cart.

Mother Courage   I thought we could find her a husband.

The Cook   Are you kidding? With that scar? The woman is dumb. She's not young any more.

Mother Courage   Keep your voice down.

The Cook   It hardly matters if I say it loud or soft. I can't have her at the inn. Because people hate looking at things like that. The face. You can't blame them for that.

Mother Courage   I told you, be quiet.

The Cook   Look, the lights are coming on in the vicarage. Let's try a song.

Mother Courage   How can she pull that cart by herself?
She's scared of the war. She's terrified. I can hear her
groaning at night. I dread to think what she sees in her
dreams. You know, after all these years she still suffers from
pity. The other day I found her nursing something. It was a
hedgehog, been crushed in the road.

The Cook   Anna, the inn is too small.

He calls out.

Now ladies and gentlemen, we shall perform for you the
Song of Solomon, and of other great men who came to grief,
so you shall know that we, too, are law-abiding people
suffering grievously in this terrible winter of plague and
famine.

He sings.

> Solomon of course was a very wise person
> There's nothing that Solomon did not understand
> But it still didn't stop his wife from departing
> And seducing every boy in the band
>
> Oh, it all ended badly for Solomon
> That's something which nobody can doubt
> Wisdom's a wonderful thing no question
> But no question you're better without.

You see, gentlemen, it's all very well to be wise but isn't it
better just to live a nice life and eat your breakfast, like
maybe some hot soup, for instance, for example?

> Caesar of course was a very brave general
> But his life ended in the utmost dismay
> With twelve knives in his back, an undignified melée
> And a scream of 'Et tu Brute'
>
> Oh, it all ended badly for Caesar
> That's something which nobody can doubt
> Courage is a wonderful thing no question
> But no question you're better without.

(*Under his breath.*) They're not even looking.

Socrates of course was a most original thinker
He did the questions and then he did the retorts
But they still got a big cup of hemlock
And put an end to his most brilliant thoughts

Oh, it all ended badly for Socrates
That's something which nobody can doubt
Honesty's a wonderful thing no question
But no question you're better without.

Right, that's wisdom, that's courage, that's honesty. What
else turns out to be not much use? Oh yes! Charity!

St Martin, of course, was a most caring geezer
He came upon a suffering tramp in the snow
He gave him his coat out of pure generosity
And they froze together, both in one go

Oh, it all ended badly for St Martin
That's something which nobody can doubt
Charity's a wonderful thing no question
But no question you're better without.

And so it is with us, gentlemen. We're good people, we keep
to ourselves, we hurt no one. And yet here we are, trapped in
a vicious spiral of despair, with – to coin a phrase – no *soup*,
and all too well aware that virtue doesn't pay, only
wickedness. Moral:

The world, of course, is full of God-fearing people
They try to live their lives in a way which is just
Yet these very same decent God-fearing people
End up with nothing but ashes and dust

Oh, it ends badly for the God-fearing
That's something which nobody can doubt
Love of God's a wonderful thing no question
But tell me, I ask you one final question
Aren't we really better without?

Voice (*from above*)   Hey you! Come on up! There's some hot
soup for you.

82

Mother Courage Cooky, I couldn't eat it. You and I, we've always understood one another, and what you just said . . . well, I know why you say it. So I have one question only. Is that your last word?

The Cook My last. Think it over.

Mother Courage There's nothing to think over. I can't leave her here.

The Cook I'm not inhuman, Anna, but the inn is small. You're making a terrible mistake. And now we must go up, or we'll get nothing here either, and we'll have sung in the cold for no reason.

Mother Courage I'll get Kattrin.

The Cook No. Bring some down to her. If they see three of us, they'll change their minds.

They go out. **Kattrin** *climbs out of the cart with a bundle. She looks round to make sure the other two have gone. Then on one of the wagon wheels she lays out a skirt of her mother's and a pair of* **The Cook***'s trousers, side by side, and easily seen. Just as she finishes and makes to leave with her bundle,* **Mother Courage** *returns with a plate of soup.*

Mother Courage Kattrin! Stay there, for goodness' sake! What on earth's going on?

She examines the bundle.

She's packed. Were you listening? Didn't you hear me? I told him to stuff his rotten inn. The inn's no use to us, we can still get this war to work for us.

She sees the skirt and trousers.

You are a stupid girl, Kattrin. What if I'd seen that and you'd already gone?

She holds onto **Kattrin** *who is trying to get away. Then she forces soup into her mouth.*

And don't imagine it was for you I sent him packing. It was the cart. I'm not ready yet to lose that cart, I'm used to it. It wasn't you, it was the cart. We'll put Cook's things here where he'll find them, the idiot.

She gets up on the cart and throws down a few things near the trousers.

That's it! Out of our lives for ever. And I'm never having another man on the cart. Now let's get going. This winter will pass, like all the others. Hurry up, it looks like snow.

They have got into harness, and now turn the cart round. They go.
The Cook *comes back, still eating. He looks at his things, dazed.*

10   On The Road. 1635.

Mother Courage *and* **Kattrin** *are pulling the cart down a country road. They come to a farmhouse. Inside a* **Voice** *is singing. They pause to listen.*

The Voice
   You plant a rose in March
   You see it grow
   A garden blooms
   It's what a home is for
   The seed becomes the bud
   Becomes the flower
   The blossom fades
   In time you plant some more

   The seasons change
   The roof you made in June
   Come November
   Protects you from the snows
   You're safe
   You watch the blizzards
   Through the winter

Home is where the heart is
Home is where the heart is
Goodness knows.

Like damned souls, **Mother Courage** *and* **Kattrin**, *having
listened, move on.*

11   Halle, Saxony. 1636.

The cart is now battered, almost finished. It is standing near a
Peasant*'s house which has a huge thatched roof and which backs onto
a wall of rock. It is night. Out of the wood come a* **Lieutenant** *and*
Three Soldiers, *heavily armoured.*

Lieutenant   No noise at all. If anyone yells, run him
through.

First Soldier   But we're going to have to knock, if we want
a guide.

Lieutenant   Knocking's all right. Knocking sounds natural.
It could just be a cow moving about.

The **Soldiers** *knock on the door of the farmhouse. The* **Peasant's
Wife** *opens the door. At once they put a hand over her mouth. Two*
Soldiers *go in. The* **Lieutenant** *points at* **Kattrin** *who has
appeared from the cart.*

Lieutenant   There's another one there.

A **Soldier** *drags* **Kattrin** *out.*

Lieutenant   Is this everyone who lives here?

Peasants   This is our son. That girl is dumb. Her mother's
gone into town buying things. She's in business. People are
fleeing and selling cheap. The two of them are just passing
through.

Lieutenant (*threatening with the spears*)   I warn you, the slightest noise and you get this through your throat. We need to know the path which leads into town.

He points to the **Peasant's Son**.

You! Over here!

Peasant's Son   I don't know the path.

Second Soldier (*grinning*)   He doesn't know the path!

Peasant's Son   I don't help Catholics.

Lieutenant (*to the* **Second Soldier**)   Show him the blade.

The **Peasant's Son** *is now forced to his knees by the spear.*

Peasant's Son   I'd rather die than tell you.

First Soldier   I think I know what might change his mind. (*He has moved across to the cowshed.*) Two cows and a bullock. If you don't tell us, then your cattle will be killed.

Peasant's Son   You can't.

Peasant's Wife   Not the cattle. Please. We'll starve.

Lieutenant   It's up to him.

First Soldier   I'm going to start with the bullock.

The **Peasant's Son** *turns to the* **Peasant**.

Peasant's Son   Do I have to do it?

The **Peasant's Wife** *nods.*

Peasant's Wife   And thank you, bless you, bless you, good Lieutenant, for sparing us, for ever and ever, amen.

These are ritual habits of deference. The war has gone on a long time and she has said this sort of thing many times. She would go on but her husband restrains her.

First Soldier   Now how did I guess what mattered to them most?

The **Peasant's Son** *leads the* **Soldiers** *and the* **Lieutenant** *away.*

Peasant   I wish I knew what they wanted.

86

Peasant's Wife Perhaps they're just scouts. What are you doing?

He is setting a ladder against the roof and climbing up it.

Peasant I'm seeing if they're alone.

He looks down from the roof.

There's something in the wood. It's moving. Right up to the quarry at the back. And men in armour in the clearing. There's a cannon. There's more than a regiment there.

Peasant's Wife Are there lights in the town?

Peasant Nothing. They're sleeping.

He comes down.

If they reach the town, they'll kill everyone in sight.

Peasant's Wife The sentries are bound to see them.

Peasant They must have killed them already, or they'd have sounded their horns.

Peasant's Wife If there were more of us, we'd have a chance. Can we do anything?

Peasant Nothing. God have mercy on them all.

Peasant's Wife If we ran down there . . .

Peasant The hillside is full of them. Maybe, if we gave some sort of signal . . .

Peasant's Wife They'd come and kill us right off.

Peasant You're right. There's nothing. It's out of our hands.

The **Peasant's Wife** *turns to* **Kattrin**.

Peasant's Wife Pray, poor creature, pray. There's nothing we can do to prevent the bloodshed. Even if you can't talk you can pray. The Lord will hear you if no one else does.

They all kneel, **Kattrin** *behind the* **Peasants**.

Our Father which art in Heaven, please hear our prayer and have mercy on all those who are in the town and asleep.

Please wake them so they may go to the walls and see that the enemy approacheth with fire and with cannon. (*Turning to* **Kattrin**.) God, please protect our mother and wake the sentry, so that it may not be too late. And save our son-in-law sleeping there with his four children, spare them in thy infinite mercy for they are young and know nothing.

Kattrin *starts to groan, and the* **Peasant's Wife** *turns to her again.*

Peasant's Wife   One of them's only two, the oldest is seven.

Kattrin *stands up, distraught.*

Peasant's Wife   Heavenly Father, hear us, for we are in your hands, we have no defences. Our farm, our cattle, our town, all these are under your care for we have nothing and the enemy is at hand.

Kattrin, *unnoticed, has fetched something from the cart, hidden it under her apron and is climbing the ladder to the roof.*

Peasant's Wife   Above all, in your goodness, intercede for our children, our parents and all your creatures.

Peasant   And forgive us our trespasses as we forgive them that trespass against us. Amen.

Sitting on the roof, **Kattrin** *begins to bang the drum which she has pulled out from under her apron.*

Peasant's Wife   What on earth is she doing?

Peasant   She's out of her head.

Peasant's Wife   Get her down, quick!

The **Peasant** *heads for the ladder but* **Kattrin** *pulls it up onto the roof.*

Peasant's Wife   She's going to get us all killed.

Peasant   Stop that, you stupid cripple!

Peasant's Wife   The Catholics'll come.

Peasant   I'm going to get some stones.

Peasant's Wife   Are you mad? Do you have no pity? Do you have any idea what will happen to us?

Kattrin *goes on drumming, staring into the distance towards the town. The* **Peasant** *is searching for stones to throw at her.*

Peasant's Wife   I told you not to let this riff-raff onto our land. What do they care if we lose our cattle?

The **Lieutenant** *runs back on with the* **Soldiers** *and the* **Peasant's Son***.*

Lieutenant   I said, and by God I'll do it, I'm going to murder you all.

Peasant's Wife   It's not our fault, sir. We did nothing.

Lieutenant   Where's the ladder?

Peasant   The mad girl took it up there.

Lieutenant   Throw down that drum. I order you!

He turns to the **Peasants***.*

This is your fault, I'll kill you for this.

Peasant   They've been cutting down fir-trees in the forest. We can use one to push her off the roof.

First Soldier   Permission to make a suggestion, sir.

He whispers in the **Lieutenant***'s ear. The* **Lieutenant** *nods. The* **First Soldier** *calls up to* **Kattrin***.*

Listen, if you come down, we'll go into town together. Point out your mother and she'll be spared.

Kattrin *goes on drumming. The* **Lieutenant** *pushes him aside and tries himself.*

Lieutenant   She doesn't trust you. I don't frankly blame her. If I give you my word. I am an officer and a gentleman.

She drums harder.

Is nothing sacred to her?

Peasant's Son   It's more than her mother involved.

First Soldier   This can't go on. They're bound to hear it in town.

Lieutenant   We've got to make a noise. A noise that's louder than her drumming.

First Soldier   But you told us to be quiet.

Lieutenant   A harmless noise, idiot. We make a peacetime noise.

Peasant   I could start chopping.

Lieutenant   Perfect. At once.

The **Peasant** *fetches the axe and starts chopping a tree-trunk.*

Lieutenant   Chop! Chop harder! You're chopping for your life.

Kattrin *has been listening and drumming more quietly. Looking round upset, she now accepts the challenge and renews her drumming. The* **Lieutenant** *turns to the* **First Soldier***.*

Lieutenant   It's not enough. You get chopping as well.

Peasant   I've only got one axe.

He stops chopping.

Lieutenant   We must set fire to the place.

Peasant   That's not going to work. When they see the fire, they'll know what's going on.

Kattrin *has been listening as she drums. Now she starts laughing.*

Lieutenant   I'm not having that! She's laughing! Get me the gun, I don't care any more!

Two **Soldiers** *go off, deliberately not hurrying, not wanting the gun used.* **Kattrin** *continues drumming.*

Peasant's Wife   I've got it. Look, if we smash up her cart . . . She's nothing in the world except for that cart.

The **Lieutenant** *turns to the* **Peasant's Son***, then to* **Kattrin***.*

Lieutenant   Do it. (*Calling up.*) If you don't stop drumming we're going to destroy your cart.

90

The **Peasant's Son** *directs a couple of feeble blows at the cart with a plank.*

Peasant's Wife   Why don't you just stop it, you bitch?

Kattrin *groans at what is happening to the cart, but keeps on drumming.*

Lieutenant   Where are those bastards with that bloody gun?

First Soldier   It must be all right, they can't have heard anything or else the shooting would have started.

Lieutenant   You see! They can't even hear you down there! I'm giving you one chance. Throw down that drum.

The **Peasant's Son** *suddenly throws down the plank.*

Peasant's Son   Keep drumming! Keep drumming! Otherwise everyone's done for! Just keep going as long as you can!

At once the **First Soldier** *knocks him down and beats him with his spear.* **Kattrin** *starts crying but still doesn't stop.*

Peasant's Wife   Don't hit him in the back. For God's sake, you'll kill him.

The **Soldiers** *run on with the gun.*

Second Soldier   The colonel's going crazy. We're going to be court-martialled.

Lieutenant   Set it up! Set it up!

He calls up while the gun is erected on its rest.

Once and for all, stop drumming!

Still crying **Kattrin** *drums as hard as she can.*

Fire!

The **Soldiers** *fire.* **Kattrin**, *shot, falls forward, the drumsticks in her drooping hands. She manages one full beat, followed by a feeble beat.*

Lieutenant   That's the end of that.

But **Kattrin**'s *last drum beats are lost in the sound of cannon fire from the town. Mixed with the thunder of the cannon, alarm-bells can be heard.*

First Soldier   She's done it.

12   Saxony. 1636.

Later the same night, towards dawn. The sound of fife and drum as troops march off into the distance. In front of the cart **Mother Courage** *is kneeling by her daughter's body. The* **Peasants** *are standing nearby, hostile to her.*

Peasants   You must get out of here. There's only one regiment after this one. You'll never make it on your own.

Mother Courage   She'll be asleep soon.

She sings.

> Lullaby, child
> What you need
> I shall give you
> Lullaby, child
> What you want
> You shall get
> Dream, child
> Dream of your future
> You haven't started . . . yet.
>
> Lullaby, child
> When you sleep
> I shall watch you
> Lullaby, child
> What we have
> We will share
> Your brother
> Lies now in Poland
> The other lives . . . who can say where?

It was because you told her about your kids.

Peasant If you hadn't gone into town to do business, it wouldn't have happened.

Mother Courage Now she's asleep.

Peasant's Wife She's not asleep. You have to face it. She's dead. You must get moving. There are wolves round here. And what's worse, bandits.

Mother Courage Yes.

She gets a tarpaulin to cover the dead **Kattrin**.

Peasant's Wife Do you have anyone left? Who can you go to?

Mother Courage Yes. I've still got Eilif. My son.

Peasant Then you must find him. We'll see she's properly buried. Don't you worry about that.

Mother Courage Money for expenses.

She has covered the body. Now she counts out money into the **Peasant**'s *hand. The* **Peasant** *and the* **Peasant's Son** *shake her hand and then carry* **Kattrin** *off. The* **Peasant's Wife** *then takes her hand, bows as she leaves.*

Peasant's Wife You have to get going.

Mother Courage *goes to harness herself to the cart. She unrolls the cord which* **Kattrin** *until then had been pulling, takes a stick, examines it, pulls the loop of the second cord through and wedges the stick under her arm.*

Mother Courage I just hope I can pull this thing by myself. It should be all right, there's not much in it.

She is ready to go.

Back to business!

A regiment passes by at the back with pipe and drum. She starts to pull.

Hey! Take me with you!

As she sets off, the **Soldiers** *are heard singing:*

Soldiers

Nobody stays at war unless they have to
At the end you see the war has robbed us blind
Have you noticed? The war itself is endless
The money's being made by those who stay behind
Nobody wants to give us decent clothing
Shit is what we eat, and we've no pay
Yet who knows? Let's face it! Miracles may happen
Let's give this thing a spin for one more day

   Spring is here. The snow is melting
   The dead are gone. They're all at peace
   And what remains must now continue.
   That's us. Let's go. We're all that's left.